A Field Guide to

BOUNDARY MARKERS

on and around

DARTMOOR

Dave Brewer

Illustrated by
Peter Hones

DEVON BOOKS

First published in Great Britain in 1986 by Devon Books

Copyright © Dave Brewer 1986
Illustrations © Peter Hones 1986

ISBN: 0 86114-786-3

British Library Cataloguing-in-Publication Data
Brewer, Dave
  A field guide to boundary markers on and
  around Dartmoor.
  1. Boundary stones—England—Dartmoor
  I. Title
  333.1   CC605.G7

Printed and bound in Great Britain by A. Wheaton & Co. Ltd.

DEVON BOOKS
Official Publisher to Devon County Council
Devon Books is a division of A. Wheaton & Co. Ltd, which represents:

Editorial, Design, Publicity, Production and Manufacturing
A. Wheaton & Co. Ltd
Hennock Road, Marsh Barton, Exeter, Devon EX2 8RP
Tel: 0392 74121; Telex 42749 (WHEATN G)
(A. Wheaton & Co. Ltd is a member of the
Pergamon/B.P.C.C. Group of Companies)

Sales and Distribution
Town & Country Books, P.O. Box 31, Newton Abbot, Devon TQ12 5AQ
Tel: 080 47 2690

A Field Guide to the
BOUNDARY MARKERS
on and around
DARTMOOR

CONTENTS

AUTHOR'S PREFACE

In the late 1940s I came to Torquay from the Wirral, married Kath, a true Devonian, and now regard Devon as home. Even in the early days my wife and I were keen walkers, but quite ignorant of what was all about us on Dartmoor, other than its fascinating tors. As we learnt little by little, it gradually became clear how this high plateauland has retained so many aspects of its past.

The crosses and other marked stones had always fascinated me, and whilst the crosses have been described by William Crossing, and more recently, by others, I could find virtually nothing, other than the odd reference, to explain the many boundary stones and the purpose of their erection. Thus it was that when I came to compose an essay about Dartmoor for a competition, I chose boundary markers as my subject. The end result, after local encouragement, sundry revisions and expansions, is this book.

TORQUAY   DAVE BREWER
APRIL 1986

ACKNOWLEDGEMENTS

THE author is grateful to Mr S. H. Woods of Porchester for his helpful comments, and particularly for seeking out various points of interest in the Ordnance Survey Boundary Report Books for the years 1882-1883, reproduced in this book.

Thanks to Kath, a fellow ardent Dartmoor enthusiast, for her support, and latterly for the legwork involved in taking photographs from which the illustrations are drawn.

The author and publisher are grateful to Dr Tom Greeves for his helpful comments and suggestions, particularly on the chapter 'The Tinners'.

NOTE

The Ordnance Survey Walkers Maps (1:25 000 scale), mark only the bounds of the Forest of Dartmoor, and the parishes. Thus, whilst all parish boundary stones, or boundary rocks, are marked (with a few unintentional exceptions), only a relatively small number of other inscribed stones, of manorial or other origin, appear on the maps of this scale. Where they do appear, they coincide with a parish or Forest bound.

The old six-inch to the mile maps (now replaced by the 1:10 000 metric maps), show many more boundstones, simply marked 'stone'. The purpose of these stones is not always apparent without a visit to the site, and even the latest maps omit a number of inscribed stones.

On the sketch maps in this book, stones are shown in the following way:

⊙ Those appearing on Ordnance Survey maps of 1:25 000 and 1:10 000 (or six-inch) scale.

● Those only appearing on the Ordnance Survey maps of 1:10 000 (or six-inch) scale.

○ Inscribed stones not appearing on any Ordnance Survey maps.

The cover photograph shows the Longstone on Shovel Down, with Kestor in the background.

INTRODUCTION

DARTMOOR and its fascinating landscape is a source of great pleasure and interest to many people. Though the majority of visitors may be content simply to drive across the moor, never venturing far from their vehicles, there is a growing number of Dartmoor 'devotees' whose appetite for knowledge is reflected in the large number of new books published each year. The majority of these titles are aimed at the casual visitor. They often provide guided walks accompanied by details of historical and geographical interest, information gleaned from a few major works, principally those by Crossing, Worth, Hemery, *et al*. It is a rare occurrence for a new book to appear involving original research and dealing with an hitherto neglected subject. For this reason the publication of *A Field Guide to the Boundary Markers On and Around Dartmoor* is greatly to be welcomed.

The first real boundaries on Dartmoor were those of the Bronze Age inhabitants. Separating one community from another, these 'reaves' consist of a low wall or bank built of moorstone, now almost entirely overgrown but still clearly visible. They were not intended to prevent livestock wandering, but served as demarcation lines, some running for considerable distances, up to three miles or more in length. Andrew Fleming of Sheffield University has spent much time in researching this aspect of Bronze Age settlement, and the recently issued Ordnance Survey maps of the 'Outdoor Leisure' series for the first time detail a significant amount of such Bronze Age boundary work.

The sequence of development of this aspect of enclosures is interesting, as some of the reaves are found crossing even more ancient stone rows, for example on Hurston Ridge; and on Holne Moor a triple stone row runs alongside a major reave.

More recent attempts to delineate boundaries on the moor followed the Perambulation of 1240 in which the boundaries of the Forest of Dartmoor were defined. Later divisions involved parish, manorial and monastic bounds, along with bounds connected with tinning, quarrying, railways, etc.

The earliest type of boundary mark involved the use of natural features, rivers, tors, cairns, and prominent boulders. Rocks were sometimes inscribed, more often the feature was simply described in documents relating to the bounds. Later, use was made of suitable moorstone erected in the appropriate spot and crudely carved. In some cases, existing stone crosses and guide posts were pressed into use, serving both their original purpose and a new function as a boundary stone. In more recent times, purpose-made stones, carefully dressed and inscribed, were erected – though not all modern stones are pleasing to look at.

All such boundary stones, though varying considerably in height and other particulars, are broadly represented by three types: (i) earthfast boulders – large, natural stones, sometimes tors themselves; (ii) rough-set stones – moorstone from the locality, hastily erected and inscribed; (iii) set stones – often carefully dressed blocks with crafted inscriptions.

Invariably, where such stones delineate the line between two or more parishes or other tracts of land, the stones are inscribed with the parish initials, or name, facing into that parish. A boundary marker may declare ownership of the land, ownership of a lease, or simply define 'limits of responsibility'.

It requires only a cursory glance at the Ordnance Survey 1·25 000 scale maps of the region to see that the symbol 'B.S.' is a common feature of the upland landscape. Finding very little published on the subject, the author set about gathering together information, both from published sources and through a great deal of fieldwork. The resultant book serves as an introduction to a subject for which no other popular study exists. It is essentially a field guide for anyone who wishes to take up the search for themselves, for there is still a great deal to discover.

Some of the information contained in this work previously appeared in a booklet published privately by the author in 1985. The illustrations are based upon the author's original sketches and photographs. Though not indicating the relative size of the stones, the drawings are executed to show clearly the inscriptions, something even the best photographs fail to capture in many instances.

Siward's, or Syward's Cross

1

The Forest of Dartmoor

THE Norman Conquest and its aftermath had a major effect on the whole of Britain, with the compilation of the Domesday Book being a major landmark in historical documentation. A recent edition (1985) of the Devonshire section of Domesday is so large that it is published in two volumes.

Besides allocating numerous manors within the county to his knights, William I designated the Forest of Dartmoor a royal hunting domain, land traditionally held by the heir to the throne who now automatically inherits the title 'Duke of Cornwall'.

The bounds of this Forest, more properly called a chase, is one of the earliest and most important boundaries, and was first fixed in 1240 when the original 'perambulation' of the bounds took place, that is to say physically walking or riding the bounds from one fixed point to the next until reaching the starting point once again.

The points of reference of the Forest were almost entirely natural features, rivers, tors, rocks, etc., together with Bronze Age remains such as cairns and menhirs. But even in 1240 Siward's Cross (marked as Nun's Cross on the Ordnance Survey), a handsome cross of some seven feet in height, was already standing where it is today, marking an even earlier boundary.

The perambulation of 1240 gave the following points of reference (the names given in 1240 are in italic, and names in the perambulation of 1608, along with the present-day forms, appear in brackets):

> *Hogam de Cossdonne* (the height of Cosdon or Cawsand Beacon, though this has long been outside the Forest bound); *Parva Hundetorre* (Little Houndtor); *Thurlestone* (Thirlstone or Watern Tor); *Wotesbrokelakesfote* (Whoodelake, Hughlake); *Heighestone* (Hingeston or Highstone, probably Manga Rock); *Langestone* (the Longstone on Shovel Down); *Turbariem de Alberysheved* (Turfehill, Metheral Common previously called Alber); *Wallebroke* (the North Wallabrook one of the heads of the Bovey); *Furnum Regis* (King's Oven,[1] remains of an ancient Royal tin smelting house near the Warren House Inn); *Wallebrokeshede* (Wallabrook head just below King's Oven); *Wallabroke usque cadit in Dertam* (Wallabrook as far as its fall to Dart – East Dart); *per Dertam usque adaliam Dertam* (to the other Dart – West Dart); *per aliam Dertam ascendendo usque Okebrokysfote* (up the West Dart as far as the O Brook); *ascendendo Okebroke usque ad la Dryeworks* (ascending O Brook to Dryworks – Drylakes); *et ita ascendendo usque ad la Dryfeld ford et sic inde*

---

[1] *see Appendix One.*

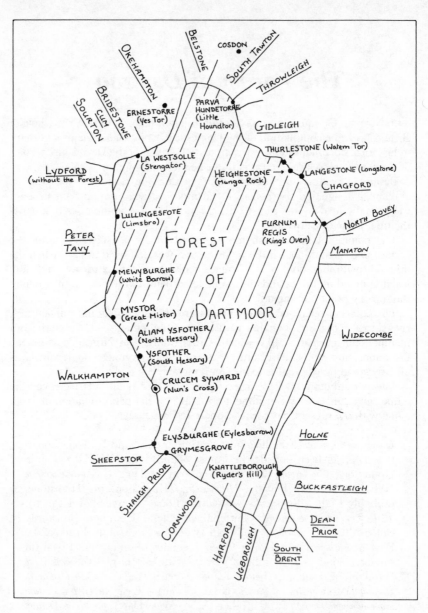

The Boundary of the Forest of Dartmoor

showing some of the prominent features mentioned on the first Perambulation of 1240 with the names given to them at that time together with the names in current usage, and the apportionment of this boundary with the 22 Parishes which have a boundary in common with the Forest

2

linealita usque ad Battyshull (thence to Crefeild fford – Dryefeild ford – and from thence to Knattleburroughe which they take to be the same that is called in the old records Gnatteshill – this latter now called Ryder's Hill); *Caput de Wester Wellabroke* (West Wallabrook head); *Wester Wellabroke usque cadit in Avenam* (West Wallabrook to it's fall into the Avon); *Ester Whyteburghe* (Eastern Whittabarrow – no longer within the Forest – the present boundary is from the Avon to Western Whittabarrow); *Redelake* (Redlake); *Grymsgrove* (1608 Arme headd – the A/head stone at the head of the Erme); *Elysburghe* (Eylesbarrow cairn); *Crucem Sywardi* (Siward's Cross – Nun's Cross on the O.S.); *Ysfother* (Hisworthy – South Hessary); *aliam Ysfother* (another Hisworthy – North Hessary); *Mystor* (Great Mistor – Mistorpan), *Mewyburghe* (White Barrow); *Lullingesfote* (Limsboro cairn near Lynch tor); *Rakernesbrokysfote* (Rattlebrook foot); *la Westsolle* (Stengator); *Ernestorre* (Yes Tor – not now in the Forest); *vadum proximum in orieltali parte Capelle Santi Michaelis de Halgestoke* (east of Saint Michael's chapel); *Hogam de Cossdonne* (height of Cosdon).

It will be seen that much of the bounds consist of rivers and streams, other points being marked on the sketch map on page 2, as cairns, tors and various man-made objects.

The twenty-five jurors of 1608 specified additional points not mentioned in 1240, including Plym Head and Sandy Ford on the Okement. Over the years

'Arme headd' 1608 – 'Grymsgrove' 1240

3

some changes have occurred, certain areas having been in dispute between the Duchy and the Commoners. Both the 1240 and 1608 perambulations specifically mention Eastern Whittabarrow but this is now totally excluded, the line in this part now going from the Avon above West Wallabrook foot to Western Whittabarrow. Eastern Whittabarrow was first on the Forest bound in 1240, omitted in 1344, but mentioned again in the 1608 perambulation. The Duchy now accepts the line from Huntingdon Cross to Western Whittabarrow, having erected a plain granite marker where the line comes up from the Avon to Petre's Cross, which Hemery calls 'Little Petre'.

The line taken near Erme Head has also changed over the centuries, after 1240 being taken to Plym Head and following a line similar to that taken today near Wheal Katherine, called Plymcrundla in Isabella de Fortibus's time.

In 1278 Amicia, Countess of Devon, made a grant to found Buckland Abbey. The grant reads as follows:

And all that our manor of Bockland, and our manors of Byckley and Walkhampton [which had formerly included Mewy], *with all suits and appurtances as in meadows, pastures, feedings, etc, mills, waters, fishings, heaths, moors, etc., with all liberties customs, etc. All donations and grants which the noble lady, our most dear mother, the Lady Amicia, formerly Countess of Devon, and the Lady de Lisle, acquired and gave the same* [to whit] *the manors of Bocland, Bykeley, and Walkhampton, according to the metes and bounds of the same, that is to say:*

from the Lobapilla[?], *on the west part of Bockland, towards the north, and the east by the middle course of the water of the Tavy, and from Walkhampton to the bounds of Dertmoor, on the north part of Mistor, and from thence towards the south of the metes of the regards of Dertmoor – that is to say, by Mistor panna* [Mistor Pan], *and by Hysforchres* [Hisworthys or Hessarys] *and Syward Cross* [Nun's Cross], *and Gyllesburgh* [Eylesbarrow] *and Plymcrondla* [right back entrant of upper reach of the Plym] *to Plymma, and from thence by Plymma towards the west, to Yaddabrok* [?], *and so by the bounds which surround Rydemore* [Ringmore], *and from thence, by Hurtwallen* [?], *to Smallacumba Cross* [Marchant's Cross?] *and Smallacumbalak* [Smallacombe], *and by the course of the water of Mewy, to Olyaka* [Lake], *and from the ditch to the way which leads from Plympton to Schlestor* [Sheepstor], *and so by the bound stones to Brycomforda*[?], *and by Crewecumba* [?] *and Denebrook* [Deancombe?], *to the course of the water of the Mewy, to Scholaforda...*

Other more minor changes have taken place including the line between North Hessary and Great Mistor. This was first brought to the author's notice when examining a stone beside the Two Bridges — Tavistock road near Rundlestone: at the junction of the Two Bridges road with the road into Princetown at SX 574749, there is a boundary stone very difficult to decipher and unmarked on the Ordnance Survey maps, but in the right light can be seen as 'Walk/hamp/ton—'Lid/ford', the Parish of Lydford, of course,

4

encompassing the whole of the Forest. It was apparent that the stone was some distance from the current boundary, and on reading William Crossing it became clear that this stone *had* been on the Forest bounds but was now well within it.

The Forest bounds now cross the road from Rundlestone Tor to the Great Mistor track and thence to the tor itself to the west of the junction previously mentioned. In fact Crossing refers to this 'modern' parish stone in making comment about the Rundlestone itself, indicating that it must have been on the boundary as late as the latter years of the nineteenth century when he wrote his *Guide to Dartmoor*. This boundary line was in dispute in 1881 when the present line from North Hessary Tor, through Rundlestone Tor, and straight to Great Mistor came into being, passing through some of the workmen's cottage holdings that used to lie along the Mistor track. A postcard of the 1920s shows several buildings there, and the author's wife can remember her uncle recalling going for milk at one of these small farms. Crossing mentions a stone seven feet in height that used to be directly opposite the 'Walk/hamp/ton—Lid/ford' stone. This pillar had the letter 'R' engraved upon it, but it has long since disappeared.

It is to be noted that the perambulators of 1240 gave the name of 'Sywardi' to the only cross named, but this has no connection with the only abbey extant at that time (Tavistock, founded in 961) on that side of the moor. The identity of Siward is conjectural but the cross, which bears the inscription 'Siward' (it is not clear whether it is an 'i' or a 'y') on the east face, also has a small incised cross and 'Boc/lond' on the west face. The cross was certainly named as an eastern boundary point of the bounds of Buckland Abbey after its formation in 1278.

Crossing, writing in 1887 in his *Ancient Crosses of Dartmoor*, suggests that the inscriptions are of a later date. The word 'Boc/lond' is now considered to mean 'bookland'; that is lands granted by the Charter of 1086, and is the derivation of other Bucklands in Devon and elsewhere. Several of these were similarly spelt in a thirteenth-century document, the *Testa de Nevil*.

It is known that Siward was the name of a thirteenth-century Duke of Northumberland, and Professor W. G. Hoskins in his book *Old Devon* also states that Siwards were known to be at Cholwich Town, a farmstead near Cornwood, at that time. A Charter in the British Museum relating to the Parish of Cornwood, the *Anntient deed for Cholleswich granted by Guy of Bryttavilla lord of Cornwood unto Erdryke Syward with the common ther*, is ascribed to the period 1200–1230.

Siward's Cross also appears on a very early map of Dartmoor, believed to be of sixteenth century origin, although its authorship is unknown. Dartmoor is shown as a circle with South Quarter defined, possibly for 'drift' purposes. The original map was recently exhibited at the Royal Albert Museum, Exeter. A picture of it is shown in Samuel Rowe's *A Perambulation of Dartmoor* – see Bibliography. A new article on the map by J. V. Somers Cocks, entitled 'Dartmoor, Devonshire' was recently published in *Local Maps and Plans from Medieval England* by Skelton and Harvey (eds), O.U.P., 1986.

Many of the crosses to be seen on the moor today were cast down in the period following the dissolution of the monasteries, and are thus to be found repaired in one way or another. Siward's Cross is no exception, but if we are to believe Samuel Rowe, this damage occurred in far more recent times, in the 1840s in fact. It now has the shaft bound with an iron strap, a restoration made by Sir Ralph Lopes.

Other very early boundary crosses included *Yanedonecross* (Yennadon), which may be that at the junction of the Princetown—Yelverton road, with the minor road leading to Lowery. *Smalacumbracrosse* has been put forward as being possibly that now known as Marchant's Cross, near Meavy, only recently re-erected after an accident. Eric Hemery, author of *High Dartmoor*, has stated that research into the early records of Buckfast Abbey by one of the Brothers reveals that Bennett's Cross, more correctly spelt 'Benet', just off the Moretonhampstead—Tavistock road, was an ancient boundary marker for that abbey, though it has been used also by the parishes of North Bovey and Chagford, and by a warren.

Siward's Cross is the only post Bronze Age marker used by the 1240 perambulations. However, there has long been controversy over what the perambulators were referring to as the location of Furnum Regis. As long ago as 1882 the Ordnance Survey Boundary Report Book recorded the cairn on the summit of Watern Hill as 'Burrow (Termed King's Oven by some)' – this cairn is still the Forest boundary (see Appendix One).

The perambulators of 1608 used a point of reference that they named 'Hethstone', the Heath Stone. There is some doubt as to the placing of this, and the stone now named as such by the Ordnance Survey is a large orthostat in a Bronze Age complex just to the east of the Fernworthy plantation (SX 671837). The old Exeter—Chagford—Tavistock—Truro road used to pass near here, over Hurston Ridge, and down to Stats Bridge. Ogilby, on his strip map of 1675 of this route, marks the Heath Stone here. There is also the question of the wording of the Latin text of the 1240 perambulation which duplicates the phrase 'et sic in longum Wallebroke', and appears before mention is made of King's Oven, this in a clockwise perambulation. It is said that this was a clerk's error in copying from the original. The Ordnance Survey gives Bovey Head the name 'North Wallabrook' to fit in with this duplication, but it is now generally agreed that it is erroneous.

An example of the confusion is mentioned in Cecil Torr's book *Small Talk at Wreyland*, when his father took up the matter. The Duchy tried to enclose land on Hurston Common in 1870/71 on behalf of a Bristol man to whom they intended to lease it. The Duchy claimed that both the Ordnance Survey and the Tithe maps were wrong, 'and all the inhabitants were wrong, although they had beaten the bounds, since they were young, just where their elders used to beat them'. Torr goes on to say that it seemed that nobody outside the Duchy Office knew where the boundaries were and even reference to the 1240 perambulation did not help to prove the Duchy case. Finally the Duchy lost its case and had to pull all its fences down, after having been taken to law.

The modern 'Little Houndtor' boundary is also known to be the recent

6

'erection' of a renter of the northern part of the Forest to extend his grazing, and that the 'Parva Hundetorre' referred to by the original perambulators indicated what is now Hound Tor three-quarters of a mile to the south. Whereas the 1240 perambulators took the line straight from Culliver's Steps, the line for years out of number has gone straight across Taw Marsh to the Smallbrook to the Whit Moor Stone, a stone probably robbed from the Whit Moor stone circle nearby, and which is shown in the Boundary Report Book of the Ordnance Survey, and also in this book.

William Crossing, in *One Hundred Years on Dartmoor*, published in 1901, reproduces the bounds of the Forest as defined in the perambulation of 1608, and quotes the extent of each quarter of the Forest for drift purposes as follows:

> *"Whoodelake (Hew Lake) att wch. place they accompt the North Quarter":*
> *"Wobrookefoote (O'brook foot) when the east quarter endeth": "thence to*
> *Plimheadd where the South quarter endeth" and "Luntesborowe, which they think to*
> *be the same that is called in the records Lullingesete (Limsboro cairn), and from*
> *thence Linyallie to Wester Redlake, between wch. said two bounds the wester*
> *quarter endeth".*

At each of these quarters of the Forest, together with the surrounding moor within the venville parishes,* drifts were made. The respective moormen, to whom, latterly, the moor was leased, were obliged to attend these drifts of cattle and ponies under their terms of contract.

In earlier times 'pounds' were used to contain the beasts gathered together at such times in the respective quarters, the best preserved being that at Dunnabridge, an almost perfect circle, for the Southern Quarter. Erme Pound and Creber Pound were others.

For further reading on the subject of commoners' rights see William Crossing's *One Hundred Years on Dartmoor*, pp. 67–75.

---

* Venville parishes were those parishes outside the Forest bounds which yet enjoyed certain rights of use within the Forest such as pasturage, etc. (See Worth's *Dartmoor* pp 342–7).

2

Parish Bounds

THE boundary of the Forest of Dartmoor abuts on no less than twenty-two other parishes, the boundaries of which were probably already formed by the twelfth century. The sketch map on page 2 shows where these parishes have a bound in common with the Forest, the boundary line being generally straight from one point to the next over the open moor, and more convoluted in enclosed land, and where river courses were used.

These twenty-two parishes are as follows, starting at the northernmost point and working in a clockwise direction:

Belstone, South Tawton, Throwleigh, Gidleigh, Chagford, North Bovey, Manaton, Widecombe, Holne, Buckfastleigh, Dean Prior, Brent, Ugborough, Harford, Cornwood, Shaugh Prior, Sheepstor, Walkhampton, Peter Tavy, Bridestowe with Sourton (this is common land to both parishes, the individual parish boundaries not touching the Forest), Okehampton, and also that part of the parish of Lydford that lies outside the Forest, all of which is within this parish.

Most of these parishes set up boundary stones at appropriate points to define their parish, not only defining the boundary between them and their neighbours but also along their part of the Forest bound. The majority of these are to be found marked with corresponding initials, some adding the letter 'P' for parish. Most are well-set pillars of granite, some rougher than others, but natural features, tors and smaller rocks, continued to be used and so marked. Some of these latter are included on the Ordnance Survey, others have been overlooked. One or two parishes continued to be satisfied using natural and other unmarked features, as did the Forest, and these appear to include the parishes of Widecombe and Sheepstor. Others such as Chagford, whilst erecting stones, were content to leave many unmarked.

A number of natural and Bronze Age features used by the early perambulators were later marked by parishes. Gidleigh used the Longstone, a Bronze Age menhir on Shovel Down, and also Manga Rock and the Thirlstone (Watern Tor), all these being inscribed with the letters 'GP'.

The Longstone was also marked by the Duchy with the letters 'DC' some time after the 1240 perambulation, and Chagford also marked their side with a rather crude 'C'. In all cases the inscribed letters face towards the land to which they are ascribed.

Other stones in the Kestor area marked by Gidleigh include one of two large fallen stones associated with the well known Four Fold Circle. This also is marked with the letters 'GP', in such a position that they may have been

The Longstone (SX 660857)

inscribed when the stone was upright. An entry in the Ordnance Survey Boundary Report Book of 1883 refers to this stone, and is interesting in that it showed the turning point between Gidleigh and Chagford as being the centre of the Four Fold Circle, not the marked stone. A drawing made by the surveyor showed the Four Fold Circle and the double stone row, including the two fallen end stones, these latter fallen at that time. It is quite possible that the underside of this fallen stone has a 'C' for Chagford inscribed on it.

Near the Batworthy wall is another boundstone, not marked on the Ordnance Survey 1:25000 maps. It is known as 'Cow Bridge', a most curious name but substantiated by the tithe map of 1843. It is situated near the Batworthy wall between the small beginnings of the stream and the Batworthy pot-water leat and never has been a bridge – the large main stone, roughly oval, is trigged up by small stones lifting it only a few inches above the ground. On the eastern end is a small letter 'G', hardly distinguishable from a 'C'.

In the other direction from the Longstone, westwards, towards Manga Rock, are two very rough-set stones above the head of a right bank tributary of the Stonetor Brook, and under Stonetor Hill, known as 'Two Stones' (SX 653856). The easternmost of these bears the letters 'GP', but the other is blank.

Some points used by the perambulators of 1240 and 1608, those having a bound in common with the parish of Walkhampton, were marked at a later date by an iron bar having the letters 'FB' (Forest Bounds), and 'WB' (Walkhampton Bounds) inscribed on opposing sides. Those on South Hessary, formerly Hisworthy, North Hessary and Great Mistor, are recorded in the Ordnance Survey Boundary Report Book of 1883, which fails to record a similar mark at Eylesbarrow. However, an iron bar does exist at Eylesbarrow and, as it is on the bound between Forest and Walkhampton parish, it is reasonable to assume it is of the same series. Both this on the Eylesbarrow boundary rock, and another on the summit of South Hessary Tor, have a 'cobra' shaped flattened head, and whilst the western faces of both have been eroded away, the eastern facing sides both show identifiable remains of the letters 'FB'.

The North Hessary sketch in the Ordnance Survey Boundary Report Book shows the position of the bar on the top of the tor, with two 'BS' (boundary stones) marked to the south-east – one is a blank stone (marked in the report 'BS out of position'), while the other has a crude six-inch arrowhead inscribed.

The bound at Great Mistor was originally Mistor Pan, a fine rock basin on the eastern edge of the tor, but the iron bar is shown as being sited at the centre of the main mass, in line with plain granite posts now erected on the line from Rundlestone.

Of the many natural earth-fast rocks inscribed by parishes, some of which are omitted from the Ordnance Survey 1:25 000 maps, the majority are relatively small. However, Buckfastleigh marked both Outer Pupers and Pupers Rock (SX 673674) where the line of their boundary, common to Dean Prior, changed direction. Their bound is interesting in that at one point it follows the line of a massive ancient surface working known as Gibby's Beam (SX 667677). This poses an interesting question concerning the age of both the Beam, a deep gert, and of the bound which uses it. Dr Tom Greeves, an authority on tin mining on Dartmoor, dates these gullies to the 'fifteenth century if not earlier'. However, Dr Greeves has since pointed out to the author that a description of the bounds in 1613 makes no mention of the beam, and in fact describes the bound as following a different course to the modern boundary. Thus it seems that the tinners beam-work may date from before or after 1613, though the question of why the boundary was changed, remains. Dean Prior had been the property of Plympton Priory but it is unlikely that the redistribution of their lands, following the dissolution, would have taken until the first half of the seventeenth century. (See Bibliography).

Stones not marked on the Ordnance Survey map include some of those on Holne's boundary between Ryder's Hill (Knattleborough) and the foot of the O Brook. The author has also discovered a stone near King's Barrow, at the northern end of Hameldon, also omitted from the Ordnance maps. It lies at the head of a combe running down to Heathercombe, and has been used by North Bovey parish, being marked solely with the letter 'B', as is customary with this parish.

The old custom, the 'Beating of the Bounds', observed at somewhat erratic intervals in modern times, is again becoming more regularly practised. Often on a seven year basis, the bound, or part of a bound, is physically walked by a group of parishioners, including children. In early times, when many would have been illiterate, these youngsters would receive incentives to

10

memorize the boundary marks: a reward of a penny, the 'bumps', or even a ducking, as of course, many boundaries follow the courses of rivers and streams.

In recent times the bounds beaten include Okehampton, Mary Tavy, Moretonhampstead, Lustleigh, and Brent, with Chagford soon to add their name to the list. In spite of the fact that most boundaries were created centuries ago, even now new boundary stones can sometimes be found during such beatings.

At the time of writing no less than three boundary stones relating to the parish of Lustleigh have reappeared: one at its junction with Bovey Tracey parish at Slade's Cross, another at a junction with the bounds of Moretonhampstead at East Wray, and a third on Trendlebere Down at a junction with Manaton parish where a gully crosses Lower Terrace. None of them are yet marked on the Ordnance Survey maps.

A sixtieth anniversary reproduction of the Torbay *Herald Express* dated July, 1925 carried an article headed 'Ancient Custom', which went on: 'Beating the South Bounds of Lustleigh – after remaining in abeyance for 80 years, the southern portion of the bounds of Lustleigh Parish were beaten on Saturday, the Northern portions from Wreyford Bridge to Clapper Bridge having been beaten last year'. It is not uncommon to split up the complete bounds thus, into suitable sections. In 1985 Brent were reported to have traversed their bounds from Gidley Bridge to Diptford, a matter of some fifteen miles.

On a recent visit to the Willsworthy Camp area the author noted two parish boundary stones, unmarked on the Ordnance Survey, relating to the bounds of Mary Tavy. These are comparatively recent additions, one plain, the other at the junction of three parishes, Mary Tavy, Peter Tavy and Brentor, is inscribed accordingly.

In the Queen Elizabeth Celebrations of 1977 held at Holne the bounds of the Manor of Holne were beaten by the commoners. An extract from the book published at that time, *A History of Holne* refers to this occasion: 'At the highest point on Holne Moor, Peter on the Mount, six year old Craig Ball of the Forge had his head knocked against the boundstone and, in accordance with tradition, he was presented with a penny. The last beating of the Manor Bounds was carried out on 9 June 1951 when Mrs Cooke-Hurle was Lord of the Manor and Farge Norrish the Reeve. Part of the record of that day reads in the Court Roll as follows: "the boundary of this Manor then runs from Brimble Ford in a straight line up the valley to Roundhole where there is a large boundary stone with the letter 'H' on it, thence in a straight line up to the Outer and Western Gulph to a place called Nine Stones and thence in a straight line to a place called Peter on the Mount, thence to another boundary stone called Little Anthony, and thence to another stone marked with the letter 'H' called the Boundstone."

It will be observed that each of the points mentioned, including the boundary stones, bore a name, either relating to its situation, or a name in common usage with the commoners on this ancient bound where the Forest

Roundhole, or 'Rounder's Hole (SX 665692)

Ryder's Hill summit (SX 659690).
'H' is Petre on the Mount; 'B' is
Petre's boundstone.

Buckfastleigh stone at Bourne's Pit
(SX 661692)

and the parish of Holne come together. However a number of these names do not accord with those given by William Crossing in his *Guide to Dartmoor*, and it is interesting to follow and compare these.

Leaving the Mardle at Brimble Ford up to which point the river, as is so often the case, formed the bound, the next point was called 'Roundhole' in the Court Roll. This Crossing calls, as the author and other walkers too have known it, Rounder's Hole. Ascending the gully westwards the next boundary stone is not one erected by the parish of Holne, but belongs to Buckfastleigh, thus it is not mentioned by the Holne perambulation. It is, though, on the same line, and is called 'Bourne's Pit'. Near this is another Holne stone which they call 'Nine Stones'. ... 'and thence in a straight line to a place called Peter on the Mount' – This refers to the summit cairn on Ryder's Hill, earlier called Knattleborough or Gnatteshill, where there are two boundary stones. The Holne stone stands only about two feet tall and is now loose and unsecured. It is more properly named by Crossing as 'Petre on the Mount', and bears the letter 'H'. It stands together with a taller and more regularly shaped pillar marked 'B' for Buckfastleigh, which Crossing refers to as 'Petre's Boundstone'. A modern triangulation point now lies near these two boundary stones, also on the remains of the cairn.

13

'Little Anthony' (SX 659692)

Holne Boundary Rock, Wellaby Gulph (SX 659701)

14

... 'thence to another bound stone called Little Anthony, and thence to another stone marked with the letter 'H' called the Boundstone'. 'Little Anthony' is, without doubt the boundary stone at SX 659692, a little distance directly North of Ryder's Hill. But what about the 'Boundstone'? On the Sandy Way where it crosses the Holne bound into the Forest stands both a boundary rock and a 'set' boundary stone which the author has always known as Fieldfare or Filfer Head, as described by Crossing, and which must be one and the same. The older, boundary rock is assumed to be the 'Boundstone'.

Beyond the description given in the beating of the bounds, the next boundary rock is that at Wellaby Gulph, SX 659701, now marked by the Ordnance Survey on the Outdoor Leisure map but omitted from earlier maps. Continuing down Drylakes, still in a northerly direction, there are other boundary rocks which the Ordnance Survey fail to mark. Where this bound joins the O Brook, there used to be another 'H' stone – one of the slabs forming Horse Ford on the Monastic Way, or Monk's Path. This stone was unfortunately washed away by a severe flood. The Forest bound continues from here to the junction of O Brook and the East Dart and thence to Double Dart.

Quotes made from notes made by John Andrews, the Modbury solicitor who travelled the moor around the beginning of the nineteenth century, reproduced in the *Transactions of the Devonshire Association* (Volume 73), include the following passage: 'Fifty five Boundary stones (were) erected in August and September 1803 of which 51 are marked on the opposite sides with the letters H and U'. These are on the Harford—Ugborough boundary. Other interesting Ugborough stones are the 'Outer U Stone' at Red Lake, and those near the Glaze and at Ivybridge where the name Ugborough is spelt out in full, that at Ivybridge being beside the bridge on the Ugborough side, with a corresponding stone for Ermington on the Western side.

The extremely long Ugborough—Harford boundary line from Western Beacon, where there is quite a collection of cairns, has incorporated into it the Longstone (SX 655583) and also makes use of a Bronze Age stone row as part of the line north of Butterdon Hill. North again, amongst other plain stones we find 'Hobajohn's Cross' (sometimes spelt Hobajon). This is not a cross in the proper sense, but a small pillar some three or four feet in height, having a small cross incised upon it. There was at one time a fragment of a cross on Three Barrows which used to be thought of as the original Hobajohn's, one of the boundaries of the manor of Brent. Further north again at SX 655607 there is another longstone, or menhir, on the line; this is now recumbent.

The author has only recently discovered that many of these stones were not erected on the parish bound but on the boundary of two moors as the result of a legal action between the owners of the Manors of East Hartford, which abuts Ugborough, and Langford Lester in the Parish of Ugborough. The upshot of the matter was the erection of the fifty-five boundary stones. A prime mover in this was Andrews, the solicitor from Modbury who was acting for one of the parties, a keen observer of things Dartmoor, and who

15

had travelled widely over it since at least 1788. All the information regarding the Andrews' papers is recorded in the *Transactions of the Devonshire Association* (1943), recorded there by Hansford Worth.

In the cause of his case, Andrews actually surveyed the Erme Plain area and was sufficiently of a mathematical mind to construct a map which Worth praises for it's accuracy. Andrews showed the Longstone 890 feet north of Hobajohn's Cross (Worth says that the Ordnance Survey are the only ones to insert an 'h' in the word). Andrews knew nothing of prehistoric stone rows according to Worth. To him the Butterdon Stone Row was a 'row of Bound Stones' and similarly the row from the Longstone towards the cross was a 'row of stones which seems plainly to have been intentionally laid, and probably for the purpose of a boundary'. The original complete stone row was 6280 feet long 'terminating on the south in a circle around a barrow, and to the north in a menhir'. Beside the longstone is a modern bound stone erected by Andrews and a man named Abrahams, acting for the other side in the dispute.

The bounds of the two parties in dispute were eventually agreed to take a line, not going straight from Hobajohns Cross to Three Barrows, but going from the cross to Longstone, and from thence to Three Barrows. This Longstone is the fallen one at SX 654607, not that still standing south of that point.

The ancient circular map in Exeter Museum shows a cross in this region, symbolically drawn as standing on a calvary, in the line of a stone row.

Reference has already been made to a parish bound stone with two angled faces at SX 574749 on the Two Bridges to Tavistock road near Princetown, with the inscription 'Walk/hamp/ton' and 'Lid/ford'. Others of this type exist at Merrivale Bridge, lettered 'Whit/church' and 'Walk/hamp/ton', on the now unused section of road to the old bridge below the inn; at Half Bridge on the Okehampton—Tavistock road, lettered 'Tavi/stock' and 'Mary Tavy'; and at Willsworthy Gate, the lettering on this being even more difficult to decipher than the others, 'Mary/Tavy' being just about legible on one side, the other presumably 'Lidford'.

Other stones have an individual character too, but the only one known to the author actually dated is the Ashburton stone at New House on the old road from Chagford to Ashburton, not far from Hemsworthy Gate. It lies at the foot of a wall at SX 741757, now marked on the new Outdoor Leisure map but not shown on other 1:25 000 scale maps. This stone is dated 1793. A reference to this in an earlier article on this subject included an error due to the author misreading his notes. It is *not* inverted from the road but is the normal way up. The author had climbed up on to the wall, (not a thing one should do!) to get a better angle to take a photograph. In the event the photo looked as though the inscription was in relief rather than the reverse when turned the right way up!

The earliest dated parish stone known to the author is of late seventeenth century date. It is not on Dartmoor but stands at the roadside near Chichacot Cross east of Okehampton (SX 610967). It marks the boundary between

Merrivale Bridge stone (SX 574749), lies on the disused road below the inn. The River Walkham is the bound.

Ashburton stone (SX 741757), near Newhouse (see text)

Okehampton and Sampford Courtenay, and is inscribed 'OP/B/1697' to the west and 'SP/B/1697' to the east.

Besides natural features named as a boundary point, many set parish stones have been given a name, often relating to a location, but not always so. Examples on the eastern side are: 'The Grey Goose' – at Dockwell Hole, the head of the Harbourne, at SX 697643; a plain pillar, one of a line running from this point to Small Brook, a tributary of the Avon; 'Grey Goose Nest' – a similar plain pillar near Blackslade Mire at the junction of Ashburton Parish with Ilsington and Widecombe SX 740759; 'Grey Mare' – yet another unmarked pillar near Buckland Beacon on the Ashburton—Buckland boundary; 'Hole Rock' and 'Hole Stone' – the former a natural rock having a small circular depression, the latter a set stone a few feet away with the letters 'HS', on the side of Smallacombe Rocks overlooking the Becka valley at SX 756785, etc.

There are a few stones with initial letters cut in relief (the majority are incised), but most of these are on old guide posts – the only exception the author is aware of being at the junction of the parishes of Tavistock, Peter Tavy and Whitchurch at SX 513752 at the entrance to the Collaton farms. Other stones bearing a single initial letter are not necessarily Parish bound stones – such as the 'guide posts' over Walkhampton Common bearing the letters 'T/A' on opposing faces – the old Tavistock to Ashburton track, etc.

The Ordnance Survey fell into this trap. Until the issue of the Outdoor Leisure map, they marked both a guide post and a boundary stone at Hemsworthy Gate, on 1:25 000 scale maps. This 'guide post'* ('GP') referred to the wooden finger post, and the 'BS' to the granite post on the north side of the road. This has three marked sides with the letters 'B' (Bovey Tracey), 'A' (Ashburton) and 'M' (Manaton), the three places to which the roads lead. *All* reference to this has been removed from the latest map.

---

* It is not the practice of the Ordnance Survey to mark the very many interesting late seventeenth to nineteenth century granite guide posts on their 1:25 000 scale maps, more is the pity. Found on the early roads and tracks, these provide another most absorbing subject in the realm of marked stones, the foremost authority being E. N. Masson Phillips of Totnes, who has had a number of papers published in the *Transactions of the Devonshire Association* over the years.

3

Manors

Most of the manors of the 'in Country' around Dartmoor date from Saxon and Norman times, some having a mention in the Exon Domesday Book, dated 1086.

Boundaries of these estates may coincide with those of either the Forest of Dartmoor or a parish and, where they do so, they are marked on the 1:25 000 Ordnance Survey maps in accordance with O.S. policy. There are, however, many manorial stones not on these bounds which remain unmarked on maps of this scale, though they do appear on the old six inch to the mile maps, with a few exceptions.

Within the parish of Widecombe, a large parish of some 11 000 acres, there are, or rather were, no less than seven manors, consisting of Spitchwick, Jordan, Blackaton, Widecombe Town, Dunstone, Blackslade and Natsworthy. Dunstone and Blackslade are now combined.

Widecombe parish was largely content to use natural features to define their bounds, as were the manors contained therein. The map on page 20 shows these bounds. However Robert Dymond in the nineteenth century had intended to erect a stone cross at the 'Two Crosses in Turfe' on the northernmost point of his bounds of Dunstone. Having regard to the name of the site, it was proposed that the cross should have two pairs of arms, or alternatively, that two crosses should be erected, but unfortunately, neither came to pass.

In recent years the Manor of Spitchwick has had what appears to be a surplus gate post with chamfered edges erected on the bank of the Wallabrook above Pizwell Ford. This, the largest manor in Widecombe parish, records at its Court Leet of 1896, that there were representatives of Great Cator, West Shallowford, Sherwell, Corndon, Christianhayes, Lower Cator, Middle Cator, Lake, Leigh Tor, Lower Uppacott, Middle Sherwill, Grendon, Tridycott, Uphill, Sherwill and Sweaton, on the jury, all farms within the manor. At that meeting it was proposed (presented) that the bounds be beaten on the 8 October 1896.

The only other boundary stones in this parish are those of Natsworthy, an ancient Saxon manor broken up in medieval times. Comparatively recently, in the 1850s, the then owner, the Duke of Somerset, erected many shaped and named stones to emphasize his bounds, these being intermingled with some older parish set stones and natural rocks, all of these receiving his initials 'DS' on the reverse, together with the date, either 1853 or 1854. This was the 11th Duke, Edward Augustus Seymour, 1775–1855.

Well shaped with a semi-circular head, a line of them now stretches over Haytor Down, from Green Lane to the Becka Brook, this line being on the

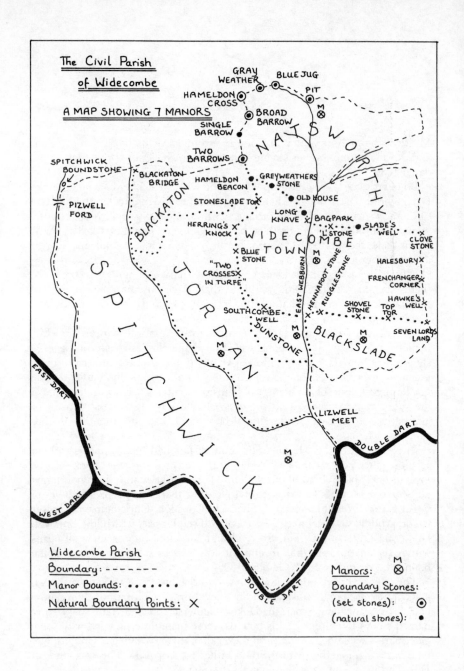

The Civil Parish
of Widecombe

A MAP SHOWING 7 MANORS

Widecombe Parish
Boundary: - - - - - - -
Manor Bounds: • • • • • • •
Natural Boundary Points: X

Manors: ⊗
Boundary Stones:
(set stones): ◉
(natural stones): •

20

One of the typical 'Somerset' stones on Haytor Down

parish bounds of Bovey, Ilsington and Manaton. From east to west they are: A stone marked 'PB', thought to stand for parish bound (Ilsington/Bovey); next, what appears to be a plain natural rock, which the author has been given to understand bears the inscription 'I.S.', 'I' the old form of 'J', the John Stone; then comes 'Prince Albert'; then Owlacombe Barrow, one of the many cairns used as a bound; the stone known as 'Old William', an old parish stone inscribed 'Wm Stone'; crossing Higher Terrace comes 'Old Jack' and 'Victoria'. Next another old parish stone stands at the junction of Ilsington, Manaton and Bovey known as 'Writenol', with the respective parish lettering; next 'Prince of Wales', followed by 'Hole Rock' and the 'Hole Stone' overlooking the Becka, again parish stones as previously described. On the Becka is 'Long Pool', marked with a crude 'LP' & 'DS' – beyond this is another at Slade's Well, though not on a parish bound, between Chinkwell and Honeybag tors.

From Slade's Well the Duke used what is known as the 'L' stone, then taking a line over to Bag Park, and up over Hameldon, running from south-east, along the spine, and then to the south-east again to the manor.

The first of these, overlooking the valley of the East Webburn and Bag Park, is a stone known as 'Long Knave', which the Duke had initialled, followed by 'Old House', another of the Duke's named stones on the remains of a cairn where there used to be a small hut. Westward there is another natural boulder, known as the 'Grey Wethers Stone' in the Court Roll of

21

Widecombe Town Manor, adjoining Natsworthy, which the Duke once again inscribed with his initials and date. Following this we arrive at Hameldon Beacon, which bears the wrongly spelt inscription 'Hamilton'. This is marked on the Ordnance Survey map, but only because of its interest as a feature, not because it is a boundstone. It is not a parish bound, the next bound to the north at Two Barrows being the junction of Widecombe and Manaton parishes.

We continue north on the spine of Hameldon to Single Barrow and Broad Barrow, both, as their name implies, are the remains of cairns. Hameldon Cross is the next, once more marked on the Ordnance Survey as a feature and as the boundstone both to Widecombe and Manaton parishes. The Duke marked this 'HC/DS/1854'. Its original purpose is not recorded but it may well be that it marks the boundary of the original manor.

Hameldon Cross (SX 704801)

The boundary turns eastwards at this point to the head of the East Webburn, where there are two more of the Duke's stones. The first we meet from Hameldon Cross is 'Gray Weather' which the Ordnance Survey persist in calling 'Grey Wethers'. The location of the true 'Grey Wethers' stone is given above. The other stone in this area is a boundstone, curiously named 'Blue Jug'.

Several years ago, whilst looking for one of the Dartmoor 'postboxes', this depicting a blue jug, the author discovered in this area a piece of molten metal, quite light for its size and probably an aluminium alloy. This may have come from the WWII aeroplane which crashed in the vicinity, and which is commemorated on a stone lower down towards the manor, very near the Natsworthy—Headland track at approximately SX 715805. This stone bears the initials of all the crew who perished from 49 Squadron in March 1941.

Moving down to 'Pit' we reach the last of the Duke's stones just off the Natsworthy—Widecombe road.

Blachford Manor near Cornwood is another ancient manor mentioned in the Exon Domesday Book. Having been in the same family since 1694, it has now been on the market twice within twelve months, offering fishing on both the Erme and the Yealm which are on its bounds.

This manor marked some of its bounds in medieval times and perhaps the best known of these is Broad Rock, a natural boulder on the so called Abbot's

Broad Rock (SX 619673)

BMAD-C

Langcombe Hill (SX 618658)

Near Yealm Head (SX 615655)

24

Way, which is also on the Forest bounds at SX 619673, above Erme Head on the divide between the Erme and the Plym. It is inscribed 'BB/Broad Rock', the 'BB' standing for Blachford Bounds. Other Blachford markers are to the south and west of this.

Those on the Cornwood parish bound are marked on the Ordnance Survey 1:25 000 maps, and these are at SX 620663 near Langcombe Head, and SX 618658 on Langcombe Hill (inscribed 'BB'). Another, at SX 615665, and inscribed 'B/L/P', denotes Blachford, Lee Moor and Penn Moor. Near Yealm Head is yet another (not marked on the Ordnance Survey), slightly below the Head where the stream Bledge Brook and Blachford Bottom run to the Erme. It is also inscribed 'BB'.

It is known that there used to be a bound stone beside the road near Tolchmoor Bridge over the Tory Brook. This was before the whole area became inundated with china clay waste. The stone was marked 'C/PM' (Cholwich and Penn Moor). A little further up the brook was another stone marked 'L/P/BB' similar to the one referred to above.

Cholwich Town nearby, is also an ancient manor, going back to Saxon times, and to which reference has already been made in relation to the origin of the name 'Sywardi'. Shell Top itself has an incised cross and has also been used as a boundary. Below to the west is a Bronze Age menhir, known as The Leaning Rock or The Hanging Stone (SX 587637). This bears the initials 'CB' – which may refer to Cholwich, though this is not known for certain.

The Manor of Brent marked its bounds in the mid sixteenth century when Sir William Petre had four crosses erected. Sir William had been a signatory to the dissolution of Buckfast Abbey in 1539, when it was valued at the princely sum of £464-11s-2d. Following this he purchased land formerly belonging to the Abbey, and in order to ascertain his title to rights on parcels of land on Dartmoor, he had a search made in the Abbey Cartulary.

It was ascertained that in 1531 Sir Thomas Denys, Sir Philip Champernowne and others, investigated whether the moors occupied by the monks were part of their manors, and the verdict was that 'the three moors called South Holne, Buckfast and Brent be parcel of the Abbot's Manors'.

Of the four crosses, only one now survives intact. This is at the junction of the West Wallabrook and the Avon, Huntingdon Cross (SX 665662). It is recorded that this once bore an inscription, but no trace of this remains.

Petre's Cross exists in a mutilated condition on the summit cairn of Western Whittabarrow (SX 654655). The cross, used by workers in the mid nineteenth century as a lintel for a fireplace that they built in a shelter on this cairn, is now minus its arms. Though replaced in an upright position unfortunately it is inverted, so that today the viewer sees not the remains of the cross head but the base of the shaft!

A third possible survivor is that which was situated on Three Barrows SX 653626. Fragments of what was thought to be the head have been seen at various times, the last sighting reported in 1957. However, the author has

Huntingdon Cross (SX 654655). Boundstone of the Manor of Brent.

seen a photograph of this 'sighting' and it is unlikely that the fragments depicted represent this cross, although one certainly stood on this site at one time.

The fourth stood at Buckland Ford, a little higher up the Avon than Huntingdon Cross, above the right bank. No remains of this cross are known. Harry Starkey writing in *Dartmoor Crosses* speculates whether these four crosses were perhaps purpose-made for the Brent boundstones, or if they were crosses of pre-dissolution days pressed into service for that purpose.

The Haytor area is rather looked down upon as being a 'grockle spot' as some put it, but there is far more of interest to the student of Dartmoor than is ever appreciated by the casual visitor. Bronze Age remains include the solitary farm under the northern slopes of Rippon Tor; Foale's Arrishes with its various stages of usage from Bronze Age times, again including a small farmstead; and Emsworthy Farm with its ruined longhouse. More recent remains include the Haytor quarries and the Haytor granite tramway, and to the south of Haytor the Emsworthy and Bagtor Mines, and the tramway of above one and a half miles in length associated with these enterprises of the nineteenth century. But in addition to all this, within a mile or so of Haytor, there is possibly the most comprehensive range of boundary markers associated with manors to be found anywhere on the moor.

We have already looked at the boundstones of the Duke of Somerset representing Natsworthy Manor on Haytor Down in the nineteenth century.

26

Another is Dunstone Manor. Reference has already been made to Robert Dymond's intention to erect a double-armed cross at the most northerly point of this manor in the latter part of the nineteenth century, shortly before he died. This was to be at the spot where stood the 'Two Crosses in Turfe', described in the Court Roll of Widecombe Town Manor. This point is a common bound of Dunstone and Widecombe Town manors, and is now marked by a plain granite post at the crest of Southcombe Hill opposite Wind Tor.

Another well known boundmark of Dunstone is 'Stittleford's Cross'. This is to be found near Hemsworthy Gate, a local name for which is White Gate. Before cattle grids were introduced this gate separated the commons of Widecombe and Ilsington, and the old granite posts of the gate are still lying where they were discarded by the roadside. In an angle of, and at the junction of walls on the Rippon Tor side of the road to Ashburton, and only a few yards from the gate, there is, built into the wall, an upright stone some three and a half feet in height, bearing the inscription 'RM', surmounted by a small incised cross. William Crossing writing in 1887 in *Ancient Crosses of Dartmoor*, states that these letters referred to 'Rawlin Mallock, who laid claim rather more than a century ago to the Lordship of the Manor'.

The Mallocks were Exeter merchants who bought the manor of

Manor bound near Hemsworthy Gate (SX 742761)

27

Cockington in Torquay in 1654 from the Cary family. The second son, Rawlyn (or Rawlin), was the first of a line of twelve generations to occupy Cockington Court. The eighteenth century Rawlyn Mallock (the fourth) would appear to have been the purchaser of Dunstone, and the instigator of the erection of what we now know as Stittleford's Cross sometime between the middle and latter part of the eighteenth century. Stittleford's Cross does, incidentally, appear as Stentiford's Cross on the Ordnance Survey map of 1906 and on the Ilsington Manor records of 1835.

A correspondent of the author who has connections with Dunstone relates that his family found a solicitor's letter to 'Charles, son of Rawlyn Mallock' pointing out the imminent sale of the adjoining manor of Jordan. This would appear to be Charles Herbert Mallock, who succeeded his father, Rev. Mallock who died in 1846. Thus it is suggested that the letters 'MR' found on Wind Tor might denote a strengthening of the marking of Dunstone's bounds at that time.

From Stittleford's Cross a line of unmarked boundstones run into the head mire of the Blackslade, these being on the Widecombe—Ilsington Parish bounds, with that of Ashburton meeting them at the most southerly bound stone, which is known as the 'Grey Goose Nest' (SX 740759).

Following this line in a southerly direction we come to Blackslade Ford. Here bridging the Tunhill track are a series of bound stones stretching to Buckland Beacon and beyond, on the Buckland—Ashburton parish bounds.

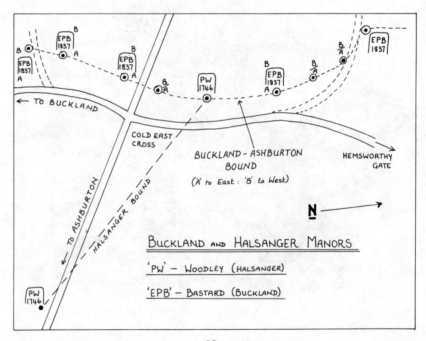

28

Edmund Pollfexen Bastard of Buckland – one of a series of his boundstones on the
Buckland–Ashburton parish bound.

The first of these east of the ford is on the scant remains of a cairn, and bears the respective letters 'A' and 'B' along with the inscription 'EPB/1837', as do several others in this line. These refer to Edmund Pollfexen Bastard, Lord of the Manor of Buckland at that time, and who also acquired the Ausewell Estate.

Beyond the stone known as The Grey Mare, near Buckland Beacon with it's inscribed tablets, are two more boundary stones. They stand in private grounds where the line decends through Ausewell Woods to the Dart gorge. The higher stone is known as Kingshead, and bears the inscription 'Kingshead May 4th 1837 A.B.'. The other is near Lover's Leap, and is known as such.

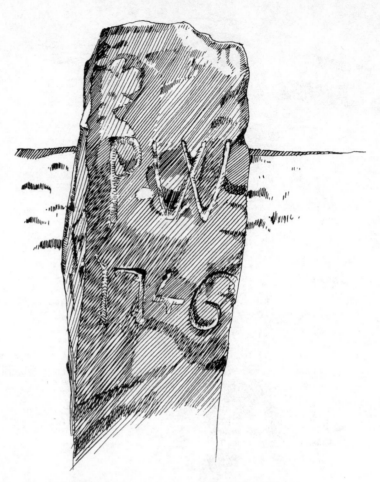

Philip Woodley manor bound (SX 744742) at Halsanger

Also along this line of stones is one lettered 'PW/1746' at SX 739745. This is at the point where the Manors of Buckland and Halsanger meet, the initials being those of Philip Woodley of Halsanger. A similar stone, which is not on the Ordnance Survey map 1:25 000 as it is not on a parish bound, can be found at SX 744742. The Woodley family held this manor for nearly 350 years from 1586 to 1925, and are believed to have had a hand in the erection and subsequent demolition of the old inn at New House, on the once busy Chagford—Ashburton drovers road.

Near Hemsworthy Gate there is a very fine cairn circle, recently cleared by the Park Authority, and known as Seven Lords Land Cairn. This is reputed to be where the lands of seven manors once came together. The wall running beside this cairn circle is the Widecombe—Ilsington parish bound, and also

30

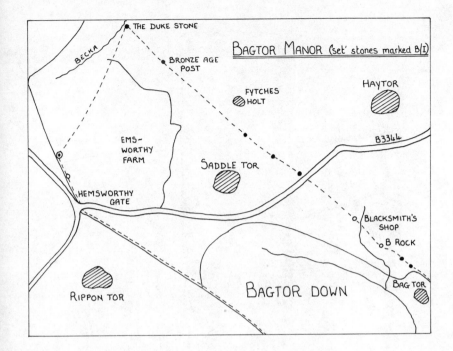

represents one of the bounds of Bagtor Manor, another ancient manor
mentioned in the Exon Domesday Book, where it was known as 'Bagathora'
and the family 'de Baggetorre'.

The house itself is tucked well under the small tor of the same name, Bag
Tor. Did the tor take it's name from this ancient manor or vice versa?
Although of no great height – about 1150 feet – and of no great prominence
from any angle, the tor is yet of interest if only for the very fine rock basin
which has now penetrated a layer of the granite to allow water to trickle out
between the top layer of rock and the next.

The settlement itself is a steep 350 feet below the tor and to the south-east,
taking water from the Sig, as did the leat to the mill a further quarter of a mile
away. But old as the manor is, there remains a stone on the verge of Mill
Wood indicating a far earlier occupation. This now serves as a humble
gatepost and bears, on one of its edges, an inscription consisting of a number
of lines similar to oghamic script, possibly of Christian Celtic origin. It is
thought possible that the stone is a memorial to a wandering Irish Saint of
around A.D. 600. A more likely theory is that it is a boundstone, on the
boundary line defined in a Charter of 1050, the Peadington Charter. Susan
Pearce refers to this in an article entitled 'Early Medieval Land use on
Dartmoor and its Flanks' (*Devon Archaelogy*, 1985). The Charter defined a
boundary following the southern edge of the parishes of Buckland in the
Moor, Ashburton and Bickington on the eastern side, very near the site of the

31

Gatepost with Celtic inscription (SX 743764)

stone mentioned above. Other early marked stones of around this period
(A.D. 600) are similarly placed on the fringes of the cultivated land, as at
Buckland Monachorum, Lustleigh, Fardle and Sourton Cross. Another has
just been erected on Sourton Common – a very recent find.

Ruins of the old Bagtor Barton remain, with the present manor house, built
around 1700, close by. The manor was the home of the Fords, and is the
birthplace of the Elizabethan dramatist, John Ford (b. 1586), baptized at
Ilsington, the parish church. His mother is buried there, and set into the floor
near the font is her gravestone bearing the inscription 'In Memory of
Elizabeth Ford, Died 1628, wife of Thomas Ford of Bagtor'.

There is a fascinating story regarding the damage to this stone. At the time
of the Civil War the Royalists, including three Regiments of Lord
Wentworth's Horse, had camped at Bovey Tracey. On the 9 January 1646
they were surprised by Cromwell and his parliamentarian troopers. Routed,
some of the Royalist cavalry made for Ashburton, others finding themselves
at Ilsington. There they made use of the church as a refuge, including their

horses, and it is believed that the imprint made on Elizabeth's gravestone is that of a hoof of one of these animals. The Fords themselves were strong Royalists, and in a later generation another John Ford was knighted by Charles the Second.

It is somewhat irrelevant to boundary markers and to Bagtor Manor, but the method that the Royalists employed to make their escape from Bovey Tracey makes a good story. The author has recently learned that the facts were related in a letter dated 11 January 1646, only two days after the event took place, and published on the 15 January by order of the House of Commons.

Joshua Sprigg, chaplain to Fairfax, who had at that time taken other Commonwealth forces to Moretonhampstead, wrote in 1647:*

It was almost supper time with them when our men entered the town, most of them at that instant were playing at cards, but our souldiers took up the stakes for many of their principal officers, who, being altogether in one room, threw their stakes of mony out of the window, which whilst our souldiers were scrambling for, they escaped out at a back-door over the river, and saved their best stakes.

It is thought that the stake money amounted to about £10 in silver, a considerable sum for those days.

From Bovey, Ilsington is only a matter of about three miles.

On the line of the wall beside the Seven Lords Land Cairn, and above Hawke's Well, there is one of Bagtor Manor's boundary stones, which the Ordnance Survey have recently included on the Outdoor Leisure map. In addition there is another built into the wall nearer to the cairn circle that they have failed to record. However these are but two of this manor's stones, all the 'set' stones of which bear the letters 'B/I' (Bagtor within Ilsington).

At the point where Bagtor Manor's bounds touch the Becka Brook, is a bound stone known as The Duke Stone, SX 747772. This appears on the 1:25 000 scale blue series of maps, but for some inexplicable reason is now omitted from the Outdoor Leisure Series. It stands on the bank of the Becka, the bound of Ilsington and Manaton, and is one of another series of ten points marking Bagtor's Bounds. Of these, seven are 'set' stones running from the Duke Stone, through the col between Emsworthy Rocks and Saddle Tor, crossing the head mire of the Sig, and following the Bagtor Mine gert to Crownley Parks. The sketch map on p. 31 does not show this latter stone.

The other three marked stones which are not granite posts include a standing entrance post of Bronze Age erection near the Emsworthy Farm enclosures, and another large stone in a Bronze Age reave which the map shows as a boundary rock. In addition it is known that a point called the Blacksmith's Shop was used. This is at SX 758764, a couple of large rocks forming a small outcrop at the head of the eastern fork of the Sig. A large well formed 'B' has been incised on the upper surface of the southernmost rock.

* Quoted in *Anglia Rediviva* or *England's Recovery*.

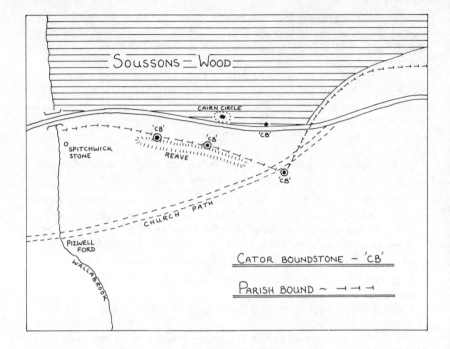

Some small stones are to be found at the base of the northern part of the outcrop, possibly the remains of a building, charcoal remains having been found here, hence the name given to this spot. It has also been suggested that it might be the site of a ruined chambered tomb.

Cator is another name to conjure with. Cator Court is, of course, the home of that indefatigable champion of Dartmoor, Lady Sayer, and there are boundary stones to be associated with Cator, which consists of not only Cator Court but Lower Cator, Middle Cator and Great Cator farms.

In this case four stones are known, each marked 'CB'. These are all situated near the southern edge of Soussons Wood and three appear on the Ordnance Survey 1:25 000 maps. These three are on the reave which forms the parish bound of Widecombe and Manaton, between the Wallabrook and the Church Path. The other is not on the parish bounds, but beside the road near Ephraim's Pinch and appears only on the six inch scale map, also quite near the Cairn Circle.

Of the farms sited beside Cator Court, Lower Cator had been, until the nineteenth century, two, or occasionally, three, holdings. The author has recently had his attention drawn to a land boundary of the thirteenth century relating to this area.

In 1966, *Devon and Cornwall Notes and Queries* (July) published an article entitled 'A Widecombe-in-the-Moor Land Boundary' by J. Somers Cocks, wherein he quotes from an ancient (undated) deed lodged with the Devon

34

Record Office. This relates to a gift of land by the then Lord of the Manor of Spitchwick, the original copy of which dates from the early years of the thirteenth century. It reads:

' ... *I Thomas de Spicwyk have granted and confirmed to Gilbert son of Leno de Cadetrew and his heirs 2 ferlings of land in Chadetrew which Michael my father gave to Leno his father with An.. his daughter and my sister in free marriage with these bounds namely: from Wedebourne as to the lands of William de Dawedunn* [Dawedunn – Jordan, at that time owning one of the Lower Cators]; *extending as far as the corner of the meadow Churtais and in line as far as the Pikestann above the back of the hill at Holeshafde* [The 'Pikedstone' still stands prominently only fifteen yards on to the moor opposite the Lower Cator track off the Ponsworthy—Bellever road, SX 684760]; *and in line to the lands of Warin son of Joel extending as far as the Fennie Ford* [Lands of Warin believed to be part of Sherril. Fenny Ford, a ford over the Wallabrook on the bound between Babeny and Riddon farms – SX 675759]; *and in the watercourse of Walebroke as far as the Horebrygge Ford* [name lost but at the point where the bounds of Middle and Great Cator meet – SX 674767]; *and in line as far as Didelake hafde and in line to the Pichedestann on Chokerard* [up the Deadlake stream to Deadlake Head. Chokerard (Cokers Hill). The pikedstone is assumed to have been on the green at Cator]; *and in line to the Clampitte and beside the corndych of the land of William Giffard extending as far as the Wedeburne'*. [The site of Clampitt is unknown but Somers Cocks hazards a guess that it is near Middle Cator, and that William Giffard's land was Great Cator].

Thus, with the help of Hermon French, Somers Cocks was able to identify most of the bound marks.

The fact that these bounds crossed reaves on Corndon Down is interesting but, since they are not referred to in the charter, Somers Cocks assumes that they are of a later date, and were not there when the deed was drawn up. It is equally possible, however, that the reaves predate the thirteenth century and that they were not mentioned simply because the line of boundary taken did not follow the line of the reaves.

Willsworthy Manor is situated in the parish of Peter Tavy. The site of the old manor house is indicated on the green 1:25 000 scale map but it is omitted from the newer Outdoor Leisure map of the same scale. It was sited at SX 535816 at Will. It must be admitted that there is virtually nothing to see of the manor itself today but, nearby, the old manor pound is still very well preserved, at the junction of a lane called 'Willsworthy Lane' leading out on to the moor. Though now in Peter Tavy parish, in the early 1880s the manor was in Lamerton parish. A boundary stone at SX 518840 is mentioned in the Boundary Report Book as 'Hamlet of Wilsworthy Lamerton'. The author has looked for this near the bridge on the main Okehampton—Tavistock road but failed to find it. There was much alteration in the parish bounds hereabouts.

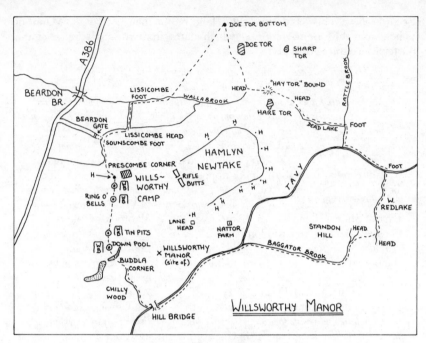

Hamlyn Newtake stone on Willsworthy land (SX 535835 approx.)

36

To quote from William Crossing's *Guide to Dartmoor*, the Bounds of Willsworthy Manor were as follows: *'From Buddla Corner on Black Down, by the bondstones running by Down Pool, Tin Pits, and the Ring o' Bells to Prescombe Corner; thence to Sounscombe Head and Sounscombe Foot and Beardon Gate; thence to Lissicombe Head and down the hill to Lissicombe Foot; thence to Greenwell, and across the marsh to the Walla Brook, and up that stream to a Bond mark in Doe Tor Bottom; from Walla Brook Head to a cairn between Hare Tor and Sharp Tor; thence to Dead Lake Head and so down to the Rattlebrook; thence to the Tavy, and up the Tavy to Red Lake Foot; up Red Lake nearly to the head, and thence to a pile of stones; thence to the head of the Baggator Brook, and down the brook by Bagga Tor farm and the Hare's Double to the Tavy; thence down the Tavy to Hill Bridge, and up by the stream on the edge of Chilly Wood to the enclosures, and thence to Buddla Corner'.*

The Manor, now taken over by the Ministry of Defence, has 'set' boundary stones which fall into two distinct categories: those of the Hamlyn family enclose a large newtake encompassing part of the Redford enclosures, from

Nineteenth century Willsworthy boundstone (SX 523833 approx.)

the Willsworthy rifle butts, circumnavigating Willsworthy Brook to end at the mine leat under Ger Tor. Just outside this enclosure, which in part is but a reave-like mound, there are no less than eleven rough-set stones lettered 'H', on the open moor. Another is sited near the camp.

Four more recent set stones mark the boundary over the down from Down Pool to Prescombe Corner. One of these is set on the Ring o' Bells, the small enclosure which may have been a cairn, at SX 522828. These bear the letters 'W/B', and the granite pillars bear the marks of feather and tare, and are thus post-1803 or so. Other stones in this area are referred to in Chapter 9.

One boundary marker referred to by Crossing, the cairn between Doe Tor and Hare Tor, is called 'Hay Tor Bound'. Crossing refers to an old map of Willsworthy Manor on which the names 'Great Hay Tor' and 'Little Hay Tor', are applied to Hare Tor and a lesser tor to the north. This is a corruption of an older name, Hey (high) Tor.

4

The Tinners

OTHER than farming in its varying aspects, the oldest industry carried out on Dartmoor is that of the tinners. Tin streaming, that is the collection of alluvial tin ore from the river beds, is evidenced by the merest glance at any river or stream valley on the high moor, and in the middle reaches of these streams.

Tin working has certainly been carried out on Dartmoor from the twelfth century and it is now considered quite possible that Bronze Age man also collected the ore for export to Europe. It is known that people of this period streamed for tin in Cornwall, but virtually no tin slag has been recovered from Bronze and Iron Age settlements on Dartmoor. However, the density of these settlements in some river valleys indicates there was some other form of inducement to settle there besides farming.

From early times, the tinners had their own Stannary Parliament and Stannary Laws. Devon and Cornwall each had four Stannary Towns. In Devon the original three were Ashburton, Chagford and Tavistock each named in a charter of 1305 – Plympton was added in 1328. This charter, of Edward I, defined the privileges of the miners and granted them immunity from the jurisdiction of all Manorial and Royal Courts whilst working for tin in the Stannaries.

The first Stannary Parliament recorded was made up of twenty-four representatives from each of the four Stannaries, presided over by the Lord Warden of the Stannaries. They met at Crockern Tor, near Two Bridges, in 1494. In 1510 the 'Great Court', or Parliament of Tinners met, declaring and clarifying existing Stannary Law. The Steward's Court, having come into being in the thirteenth century, was abolished by the Stannaries Court Act of 1836.

The last General Stannary Court was held at the White Hart Inn in Moretonhampstead on the 11 December (27 December, George III), 1786 and referred to the bounds of the respective Stannaries in 1613. The purpose of this meeting was declared to be the clarification of the 'Limit and Bounds of the Jurisdiction of these Courts', and to ascertain the customs of earlier times. Of the twenty-four jurors summoned from each of the four Stannaries concerned, the representatives sworn-in comprised Ashburton (5), Chagford (6), Tavistock (4), and Plympton (1).

An ancient manuscript book, said to date from 1762, was referred to, in which a Copy of the Presentments of the Bounds of the several Stannary Courts of Devon appeared, dating from 1613. This was said to include details of Bounds 'which contain some such Antient Names of places as are to them at present unknown'.

BMAD-D

The Bounds were stated as follows:

Chagford Stannary: *The limits and bounds of the Stannary Court of Chagford and the Bounds and Limits which divide the Two Stannaries Courts of Chagford and Ashburton are as followeth beginning from Crockerentor to Broken Borough from thence to Lower Cater, part of Lower Cater in the Jurisdiction of Chagford, and the other in Ashburton, from Lower Cater to a village called Dunstone, part in Chagford and part in Ashburton, from thence to the Village called Blackslade part in Chagford and part in Ashburton and from thence to a village or Tin Work called Crownellhead and so to Swine Path Cross and from thence to Stowford Bridge and so to Teingbridge and from thence to Teingmouth the water dividing ...*

The Bounds between Chagford and Tavistock are these from Crockentor North by Tavey Head and Broom Lake to the Head of a River called Ockment or Okement and from thence to the West Bridge in the Town of Okehampton and from thence North to Monkokehampton and from Monkokehampton North East unto a parish called Highbickington and to the River Taw and from thence as the same River runneth to Barnstaple and from thence unto the North sea as the Watter runneth – And further they present That all Devon lying within the Circuit and Compass of those Limits are within the Jurisdiction of the Stannary Court of Chagford and all Tin works lying within the said Bounds are within the Stannary Court of Chagford and all Tinners inhabiting in the Towns and Parishes contained within these Bounds are and always have been reputed Tinners dwelling within the Jurisdiction of the Stannary Court of Chagford and ought to be Contributary to all Rates and Musters as Tinners Inhabiting in that Court ...

Ashburton Stannary: *The Limits and Bounds of the Stannary Court of Ashburton on the North and East Parts are from Crockerentor eastwards to Riddon in Withecombe parish and from Riddon to lower Cater from thence to Rowdon, from Rowdon to Dunstone to Chittleford from Chittleford to Blackslade from Blackslade to Crownley head in Ilsington parish, from Crownley head to Swine path Cross thence to Lownston as the way leads from thence to Levaton and from thence as the way leadeth unto Stowford Bridge otherwise called Stowford Stone, between Highweek and Teinggraze, and from thence to the Middle Pier of Teingbridge and from thence to the Mean Sea as the River of Teing Runneth and on the West and South parts distinguishing Ashburton Stannary from Tavistock and Plympton Stannaries – From the said Crockerentor Southward to Broken Burough and from thence to Cranelaketor from thence to Dunagoat, and from thence to Peters Cross and from thence to threeberry, and from thence to a Stone called Hobba Jame's Cross and from thence to the Range of Stones untill you come to Butterdon Burough and from thence to Broadaford, and from thence to the Seven Stones which part several parishes and from thence to Michael Burough adjoining to the Sea, and all Tinworks lying within these Bounds are reputed to be within the Stannary Court of Ashburton and all Tinners inhabiting in the Towns and parishes within these Bounds are reputed as Tinners dwelling within the Stannary Court of Ashburton and are contributary to all Rates and Contributions as Tinners within the said Stannary and are Trained and Mustered among the Tinners of that Court on Contributary to the same ...*

40

Plympton Stannary: *The Limits and Bounds of the Stannary Court of Plympton beginning at the full sea mark at Plymouth to the Eastern End of the old Quay and from thence up the Street called St Andrews Street, and another Street there called the Old Town leaving all the Dwelling Houses over the West side and North in Tavistock Court, and so the Highway from Plymouth Northward to Uddlestor Rock (upon Roborough Downe) and from thence North Eastward to Horraplud from thence East the Way to Yannadon Cross from thence South East by Woodland Hedge dividing the parishes of Meavy and Walkhampton to Crecobye foot falling into the River of Meavy East and ascending the River of Meavy North East to Reddapit lake, and so ascending that lake Eastward to Blew Stone from thence to Horradill head, from thence South East to Broken Burough, from thence South to Market place lodge, from thence to Crannaberr and so Southward to Dunnagoat Stone in Wellake Lawe, from thence to Saint Peters Cross, and so water Shutt the same Hill to Piggow Beacon, from thence to Modbury Steeple, and from thence to St. Michaels Burrow, all Tinworks whose heads and head Wiers lie within these Bounds are reputed taken and known to be within the Stannary Court of Plympton aforesaid, and all Tinners inhabiting in the Towns and Parishes within these Bounds are reputed and taken as Tinners dwelling within the said Stannary Court of Plympton, and are contributary to Rates, contributions, Trainings, Musters and all other Suits and Impositions imposed upon the said Stannary Court of Plympton as it hath in time past been used beyond the Memory of Man ...*

Tavistock Stannary: *The Limits and Bounds of the Stannary Court of Tavistock beginning at the Old Quay in Plymouth and from thence up to the Street called Saint Andrews Street Westward, and from thence to a Street called the Old Town westward and then from the Old Town by the Highway Northward upon the North West side to Uddlestor Rock (upon Roberough Downe) from the Rock called Uddlestor Rock North East unto Horraplud, the North West side of the way to Yannadon Cross from thence North East by Woodland Hedge dividing the Parishes to Crecaby, from thence to the River of Meavy, and from thence to Reddapit lake Eastward and from thence to a place called Blewstone and from thence North East by Horradill Head, and from thence to Crockerntor And from Crockerntor North to Tavy head, from Tavy to Bromelake, and from Bromelake to the West Bridge in Okehampton, and from thence North to Monkokehampton and from Monkokehampton North East unto a Parish called Highbickington, and from thence to Tawton and so to Barnstaple and from thence unto the North Sea and all such Tinworks as lye within these Bounds extending on the West to the Bounds that divide Devonshire and Cornwall are within the Stannary Court of Tavistock and all Tinners which dwell within these Bounds ought to be Contributors and to be rated within the Stannary of Tavistock Court.**

The Stannary Law required that tinners' bounds were marked. The

---

* This information, previously unpublished, is to be found in Tom Greeves' unpublished thesis on tin mining *The Devon Tin Industry 1450-1750* (1981).

41

charter dated 1201 gave tinners the right to 'mine for tin and dig turves for smelting tin everywhere in the moor and fiefs of Bishops, abbots and Counts as they have been accustomed to do'. In 1752 a Convocation provided that 'by the common usage and custom of the Stannaries, any tinner may bound with tin bounds any wastrel lands within the County – that are unbounded or void of lawful bounds; and also any several and enclosed lands that have been anciently bounded and assured for wastrel by payment of the toll tin before that the hedges were made upon the same: and also may cut bounds in the Prince's several and inclosed ancient assessionable Duchy Manors according to the ancient custom and usage within the said several Duchy Manors'.

The 'pitching' of a pair of Bounds as described in the second half of the sixteenth century was as follows: 'The manner of bounding is most commonly to make four corner bounds, two at the head of the work and two more at the tail, in cutting up three turves in every corner, and so consequently their side and head bounds with three turves in every place, one directly against the other'. A quote from the eighteenth century reads as follows: 'they (the tin bounds) are limited by holes cut in the turf, and the soil turned back upon the turf which is cut, in form of a mole hill, and directly facing containing sometimes an acre – sometimes the bounds were marked with stones, and not turves, in order to preserve evidence of the limits of the bounds'.

Whilst these references were to tin bounding in Cornwall, it is likely that a similar system would be used in the Stannaries of Devon. Thus if much of the earlier bounding of claims were made by means of the turning of turves, it is hardly surprising that one finds so few remaining today. But groups of three stones can be found that are definitely associated with tin workings – the author has identified a very fine example by the Gallaven under Rival Tor. Like so many streams this has been turned inside out and many spoil heaps remain.

One of the fascinations of Dartmoor is that there is always something more to learn and new things to discover, in spite of the considerable amount of literature on the subject. Spoil heaps and the remains of tinners stamping mills, knacking mills and blowing houses are not unplentiful, nor are the associated mortar stones and mould stones. However bound stones are a different matter.

In the *Transactions of the Devonshire Association* 1962, under the title 'A Forgotten Manor in Widecombe-in-the-Moor', relating to the Manor of Dewdon (Jordan), Mr Hermon French refers to a document dated May 1759. It concerns an application to have proclaimed a pair of tin bounds to be known as the Dockwell tin bounds. This encompassed much of the Jordan lands bordering the West Webburn, and it is interesting to consider the size of the area bounded. It is held in the names of Roger Hannaford of Widecombe and Robert Mann of Denbury.

The bounds 'cut and pitched' on 17 April 1759, were granted in the Stannary Court at Chagford on 25 July 1759, and were described using natural features, some of which were manor boundary points, as follows:

'The Head Weare of which is is on Hambledon Hill a little under Stoneslade Tor; the first side bound east by Bluestone near Kingshead Corner; the second side bound east on Wind Tor by a stone; the third side bound east near Watergate; the fourth side bound east in a field on Quannon (Corndon) a little distance from Jordan Mill; the first side bound west near Clay Park corner (on Hatchwell); the second side bound west in a field of Blackaton called Middle Park; the third side bound west in Broadaford hill a little above the house; and the river leat and tail bound in a field of Quannanford called Bridge Park, a little below the steps'.

However, tinners 'set' bound stones are few and far between. One that is definitely ascribable to the tinners is a marked natural stone above the 'Knack Mine' near Steeperton Hill at SX 614885. This is a bound of what was known as Wheal Virgin, and the stone is inscribed 'WV'.

This stone was only recently found, as a result of papers discovered in Chudleigh and was shown to a number of walkers by Dr Tom Greeves past Archaeological Officer of the National Park, and expert on the tin industry on Dartmoor. In the *Transactions of the Devonshire Association* 1985, Dr Greeves published a very fine and detailed article on this nineteenth century mine, variously known as Knack Mine (Ordnance Survey), Knock Mine (Crossing), Wheal Virgin, or Steeperton Tor Tin Mine.

Wheal Virgin stone (SX 614885)

43

Wheal Virgin is first recorded in 1799, and in 1836 a licence was granted for twelve months by the Duchy to a mine agent and two traders, all of Tavistock, to search for minerals on land known as Wheal Virgin, with the following bounds:

'from a certain Rock or Stone marked WV on the Eastern side of the Shaft known by the name of Wheal Virgin to the length of three hundred fathoms Eastward, and four hundred fathoms Westward, being together seven hundred fathoms on the course of the lode on which the said Shaft is now sinking, and one hundred and fifty fathoms north and south thereof.'

This limited bound, confined to the line of the lode, contrasts with another made in October 1854, typical in size for Dartmoor grants, according to Dr Greeves, of some six square kilometres, under the title 'Stepelton or Steeperton Tor':

'bounded on the South by a straight line drawn from the centre of Wild Tor to the centre of Dinger Tor; on the East by the river which flows along the Eastern side of Steeperton Tor; on the north by a straight line drawn from the confluence of the last mentioned river with the river Taw – to the centre of East Mill tor, and on the West by a st. line drawn due south from the centre of the said East Mill Tor'

Through the Chudleigh papers Dr Greeves is able to refer to many invoices and other documents concerning costs, employees, etc. He records the fact that in 1877 various mine machinery was purchased (all for £65!) from the Gobbet Mine at Hexworthy:

'Stamps Water Wheel, Large Spun Wheel Shaft Bearings, Stamp Axle with frames and 12 Heads complete Buddle Water Wheel Round and Square Buddles and all Gear belonging to the above and the Tin Chest Mine Bell and Windlass, all now at the Gobbet Mine.'

In the Riddon Ridge area, within the Forest of Dartmoor, there are five stones bearing various sets of initials which are believed to relate to the bounds of tinners. One of these is on the right bank of the Wallabrook below Pizwell Bridge, amongst tinners waste. It is obviously associated with a very prominent reave leading off the left bank in a north-north-east direction at SX 672773. Here stands a rough-set stone inscribed with the initials 'FS/H'. Since the Wallabrook here forms the Forest boundary, this stone appears on the Ordnance Survey 1:25 000 scale maps as a 'BS'.

The remaining four stones do not appear on this scale map, nor on the six inch map. They all stand on Riddon Ridge itself – three of them quite close together.

The most southerly is recumbent within the centre of a cairn circle marked on the 1:25 000 maps at SX 669763. It is a fallen rough-set stone bearing the initials 'TS/H'. There is no doubt that it is a 'T' and not an 'F' as appears on

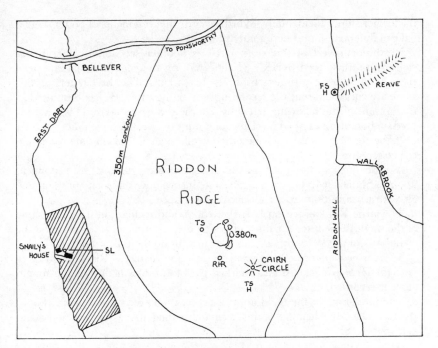

Tinners stone near Riddon Ridge (SX 672773)

45

the former stone. Incidentally, Worth records that fragments of pottery and a flake of flint were found here many years ago.

North-north-west of this cairn circle is another set stone, rather better shaped, and inscribed 'RHR' (SX 667765), on the edge of a shallow pit – there are a number of tinners trial pits thereabouts. The three letters on this stone are curious in that the second upright of the letter 'H' has been used as the upright of the following letter 'R', as the drawing shows. This device is used on boundstones at Mary Tavy, and it is possible this style points to their probable age. Certainly, such a method would save the mason time in carving the inscription.

A little further north-north-west again we come to the third stone at approx. SX 665764. This is a large stone incorporated into one of the many east–west reaves that cross Riddon. It is inscribed 'TS'.

The farm, Riddon, variously spelt Reddon and Riddam in the past, is one of the single ancient tenements and lies on the eastern side of the ridge on the right bank of the Wallabrook, and thus just inside the Forest bounds.

There is no evidence of a blowing house in the vicinity of Riddon, but there is at the farm a mortar stone, and nearby, built into a hedgebank, a mould stone is recorded.

The fifth stone in the Riddon area lies on the lower western slope, above the East Dart. It is leaning against a small building above Snaily's House and is inscribed 'SL'.

'RHR' stone on Riddon Ridge (SX 667765)

46

'TS' stone on Riddon Ridge (SX 665764)

Recently, what was obviously the site of a very productive and ancient tinners mill was excavated at Horrabridge, prior to a garage being erected on the spot. This produced a host of mortar stones in varying types of stone, a broken mould stone, etc., many of which now make a feature to the gateway of the house called 'The Tinners Mill'. The author photographed these stones, together with others in the garden, with the owner's permission, just after it had been raining, and what a variety of colours there were.

The stones in the gateway include two which are not mould/mortar stones. Unfortunately only fragments remain, but one of these bears the letters 'JB', a possible tinners bound stone. The other is inscribed with the Roman numeral X. It is known that blowing houses of the seventeenth century had to be registered and it is possible that this stone refers to this mill being Number 10.

Black Tor blowing houses are well known. Situated on the banks of the Mewy, or Meavy, blowing houses stood on both banks of the stream. That on the left bank still retains a doorway lintel intact in situ. This has the Roman numeral XIII (13) inscribed upon it which has long been speculated as being its registration number.

Worth records details of the Black Tor sett ('sett = area of land contained within the mine boundary) as follows:

1654. Lease of Tin Bounds. Sir Richard Strode, Charles Arrundle, John Bunhole, William May, John Baylaie, lease to Matthew Yandall and Roger Williams the younger, of Walkhampton, a certain tin work known as Blacktor. Bounds given and the fact that the work was a lode stated.

Between these Blacktor blowing houses and the Devil's Elbow there is much tinner's waste and the author has observed no less than three man-made features believed to be caches.

A very much more modern mine boundary stone is to be found in Chaw Gulley, between Headland and Vitifer at SX 689808.

This is the only known boundary stone bearing the complete name of a mine, East Birch Tor, and is believed to be of mid nineteenth century origin. Amid extensive and deep surface workings, the mine is sited at the western extremity of East Birch Tor sett and possibly worked the same lode as Vitifer. As usual, all the lodes here run in an east-west direction.

The author has also recently come across two marked stones bearing the initials 'SB'. One is a set stone, the other a huge natural boulder. Both lie only a few yards from the Grimstone and Sortridge Leat between Merrivale and Windy Post, the cross near Feather Tor. The large boulder forms part of a very old enclosure at SX 540748, and the rough-set stone at SX 537745, stands below the leat and not far from the site of the old Blacksmith's Shop. This section of the leat was re-routed sometime after the opening of Merrivale Quarry in 1876, and it is possible that these two stones, both about the same distance below the course of the leat, might refer to this diversion, but it has also been suggested that they may belong to the Staple Tor tin sett which is known to have existed.

John Robins, in his excellent book *Follow the Leat* – second edition – records that the Whiteworks Bounds are also known to have been marked. Bound stones are stated to have existed with the inscriptions 'W1', 'W2' and 'W3'. Despite the fact that the position of these markers was specified they have

Nineteenth-century tinners bound at East Birch Tor Mine (SX 689808)

48

Large inscribed boulder near the Grimstone and Sortridge Leat (SX 540748)

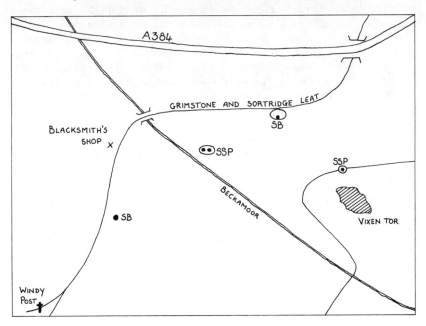

never been found. The author has recently heard from a correspondent that when a new reservoir at Swincombe was proposed some years ago, papers prepared by the Water Authority mentioned the stone W2. The correspondent added that 'a young man's father, whilst repairing a wall "over Swincombe way", noticed such a stone, but that whilst he was away from superintending the work, his workman had already incorporated it into the rebuilt wall'. Whether the inscription is now visible is unknown.

The bounds as set out in 1836, when a licence was granted by the Duchy to William Thomas and Hugh White, at 1/18 dues, were as follows:

from Torr Royal Castle Eastward following the line of the Southern Wall of Torr Royal Estate to a stone on the said wall marked W1 from thence in a straight line due south to the southern side of the Swincombe River, from thence along the southern side of the said River to a Rock in the said River marked W11 where the Swincombe and Countycombe Rivers meet, from thence South West by West in a direct line to intersect the old leat going to White Works on the North side of Fox Torr Hill, and so along West and Northward by the South side of the said leat to a Rock in Sunny Corner marked WIII and from thence in a direct line northward to Torr Royal Castle, being a Cottage in ruin at the Southern entrance to Torr Royal Estate...

Not too far from Whiteworks, on the southern side of Foxtor Mires, is yet another set stone believed to refer to the bounds of a tin mine. This is the Headless Cross, which is situated at Wheal Anne Bottom.

The Headless Cross is a granite pillar standing some six feet high, having no 'arms' but bearing a small incised cross on the north-facing side. Whether this was a cross removed from its original position remains open to doubt. It is a fact that it stands on the route of no known ancient track. A drawing reproducing a photograph taken in about 1900 by a Dr Prowse, shows a fragment of the stone surmounting the pillar we see today, perhaps flawed, or resting on the pillar as it now stands. Later, in the 1950s, Surgeon Commander Anthony and Jim Boddy's father rediscovered this fragment at the foot of the pillar, but it's origin remains a mystery. The Headless Cross is marked on the Ordnance Survey at SX 613695.

The incised cross on this stone does not necessarily prove that it was once a cross in the recognized sense. Other boundstones are known to be similarly incised, for instance Hobajohn's, and another on the east side of Kennon Hill, a Gidleigh parish stone.

5

Warrens

WARRENING, that is the breeding of rabbits for both meat and the pelt, was an important part of the Dartmoor economy for centuries. It was not until after the Second World War, and the decimation of rabbits by the introduction of myxomatosis, that it finally vanished.

Rabbits are not indigenous to this country, but were introduced by the Normans for food and sport, and multiplied prodigiously. However, Dartmoor is not an ideal habitat for rabbits in the wild, as it is too wet and badly drained, and too severe in the winter. Thus it was that they were 'farmed' on warrens, the remains of many of which may be picked out by an observant eye. The 'buries', called Pillow Mounds on the Ordnance Survey maps, are artificial mounds of stones covered with turves, and lying in such a fashion that they were drained and remained dry.

Although the word 'warren' is synonymous with 'rabbit', the following extract from *Forest Law* widens the definition: 'The word 'warren' was used to denote either the exclusive right of hunting and taking certain beasts *ferae naturae* in a particular piece of land, or the land over which such right extended.' There appears to be no specific reference to the rabbit.

The Plym Valley is, perhaps, the most extensive area devoted to this practice, embracing the warrens of Trowlesworthy, Ditsworthy, Hentor, Legis Tor and Willings Walls; others include Headland Warren at the head of the West Webburn, Vag Hill Warren on Dartmeet Hill, Huntingdon Warren above the Avon, Soussons, Wistman's, New House opposite the Warren House Inn, etc.

The warren of Trowlesworthy adjoins that of Hentor above the left bank of the Plym. It is known that a 'de Traylesworthy' was granted land on which to farm a warren as early as 1272, and Crossing in his *Dartmoor Worker* states that: 'the two being separated by an affluent of the Plym named Spanish Lake, which little stream acts as the northern boundary of the warren. Its western boundary is the Plym, and its southern the Blackabrook, the eastern being formed by a line drawn from the latter stream to Spanish Lake'.

This warren was in the region of five hundred acres in extent, but even so was not as large as Ditsworthy, which took over Hentor and Legis Tor warrens in later years.

R. G. Haynes, in his paper 'Vermin Traps and Rabbit Warrens on Dartmoor', published in the *Post Medieval Archaeological Journal*, refers to a copy of an 1807 lease regarding Hentor warren:

The Right Honble John, Lord Boringdon,
to Peter Nicholls of Sheepstor, Warrener
29th Sept 1807

Lease of some Waste on Lee Moore and an agreement abt a Warren on Hentor etc during the life of Mrs Mary Frances Penson.

Lord Boringdon granted – upon lease 'All that part parcel and portion of a certain common called or known by the name of Lee Moore situate and lying in the Parish of Shaugh in the said County of Devon according as the same is now meted and bounded out from the said Common of Lee Moore in manner following (that is to say) from a certain row or heap of stones joining Trowlesworthy Warren and Spanish Lake Head ... about Forty land yards above the same to a large Rock marked with the initials H.W.B. No1 from thence straight on East to another stone marked No2 Eighty yards above the said Row on heap of stones from thence in a straight line to another bound Stone marked No3 Which is Forty Yards South of the large upright rock in Hentor from thence to the Head of Shabbacombe Lake ... to another bound Stone marked No4 from thence in a straight line to Colesmills (formerly a Stamping mill) adjoining the River Plym to another bound Stone marked No5 ... and which said Stones are in all other respects bounded by the Tenements called Willings Walls and Hentor in the said Parish of Shaugh, etc etc'

This was a lease for a period of fifty years.

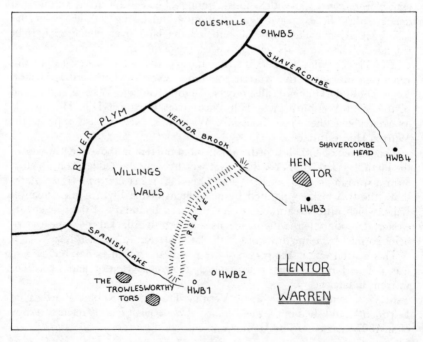

52

Hentor Warren bound 1 (SX 584644)

To take these stones one at a time:

'from a certain row or heap of stones joining Trowlesworthy Warren and Spanish Lake Head ... about Forty land yards above the same to a large Rock marked with the initials H.W.B.1 [The 'row or heap of stones' is the contour reave at 340 metres and the large boulder is in fact marked 'HW/B 1' (SX 584644). It is not on the Ordnance Survey six inch map], *from thence straight on East to another stone marked No2 Eighty yards above the said Row on heap of stones* [This is a 'set' stone some four feet in height, lettered 'H/W/B2' at SX 585645 – not due east by any means, but north of east. Again it does not appear on the six inch Ordnance Survey map]; *from thence in a straight line to another bound Stone marked No3 Which is Forty yards South of the large upright rock in Hentor* [This is another 'set' stone east of south of Hentor, smaller than No2, about three feet high and lettered 'H/W/B3'. This appears on the six inch Ordnance Survey map

Hentor Warren bound 2 (SX 585645)

Hentor Warren bound 3 (SX 595652)

at SX 595652, though at more than forty yards from the tor]; *from thence to the Head of Shabbacombe lake ... to another bound Stone marked No4* [This, a search failed to find, but is still marked on the Ordnance Survey six inch map at SX 603653]; *from thence in a straight line to Colesmills (formerly a Stamping mill) adjoining the River Plym to another bound Stone marked No5* [This also remained undiscovered after a most exhaustive search. It is not on any Ordnance Survey maps, six inch or 1:10 000 scales].

Thus three stones were found, whereas R. G. Haynes has stated in his paper 'Vermin Traps and Rabbit Warrens on Dartmoor' that only two now exist. The others may yet be found – there are recent signs of search in the area. (Another rarity recently identified, right up on the top of Shavercombe Head, was a family of black grouse.).

Other warrens on the Plym used streams entering into the Plym, and the Plym itself, as boundaries. The use of any set stones is, so far, unknown on any of these warrens.

Ditsworthy approached a thousand acres in extent in later years when it took over a number of other warrens. The bounds of these stretched up to Eylesbarrow, and up the Plym as far as Evil Combe.

Legis Tor Warren, known also as New Warren, was equipped with rabbit-proof walls on the north and west sides. Willings Walls Warren was bounded by Hentor Warren to the south, with Spanish Lake, Hentor Brook and the Plym itself on the other three sides. Trowlesworthy's five hundred acres were contained by Spanish Lake, the Blacka Brook and the Plym.

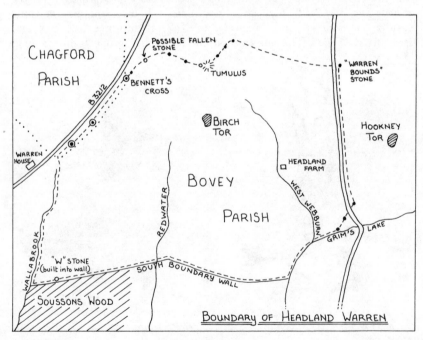

Warren Bounds stone (SX 696816)

Warren Bounds stone, southern wall (SX 675803)

Of the other warrens, Headland Warren, at the head of the West Webburn, and the surrounding area provides us with the best marked bounds of all. Dating from the 1870s, this warren embraces an area of approximately six hundred acres, this equating to about a square mile, with a series of granite set stones around its perimeter.

The six inch Ordnance Survey map shows thirteen of these boundstones, and Eric Hemery in *High Dartmoor* also mentions this number. However, the present author has noted no less than fifteen definite stones and one probable one, making sixteen in all, this including Bennett's Cross, which also served as a boundstone.

The area covered extended from the West Webburn—East Bovey divide in the east to the Wallabrook, on the Forest bounds, in the west.

The boundstones, with two exceptions, all bear the letters 'WB' – Warren Bounds – the exceptions being a stone slab on the bank beside the Widecombe—Moretonhampstead and Chagford road where a bridle path to Coombe, and now designated the 'Two Moors Way', crosses this road at SX 696816. This stone bears the inscription 'Warren Bounds'. Another, previously unrecorded, stone is built into the rabbit-proof southern boundary wall. Built into at the foot of this wall it bears the letter 'W' only, and is to be found above the Wallabrook on the southern or Soussons Wood side, at SX 675803.

Of those others marked 'WB', a couple bear the letter 'B' on the side facing east – this refers to the parish of North Bovey. These stones are within, but not on, the parish bounds of that parish. Another stone bears additional letters (see drawing) believed to refer to an erstwhile warrener. This stands beside the road near Grim's Lake.

Of all these markers, only two appear on the 1:25 000 Ordnance Survey map. These are the two that happen to be on the line of the parish bounds of

55

Warren Bounds stone near Grim's Lake
(SX 697808)

Skaigh Warren bound (SX 633933)

North Bovey and Chagford, parallel with the road near King's Oven. Bennett's Cross, which is also on this bound, is marked with the usual 'WB' on it's western face.

Vaghill Warren, situated beside Dartmeet Hill, predates many warrens. Whilst no boundary stones were erected it is known that this warren dates from the early seventeenth century, and a lease dated 1613, in the Exeter City Library Muniments, specifies the bounds. The lease was granted by William, Earl of Bath, to one Richard Reynell and Walter Fursland of Bickington, and described the bounds as follows:

> *waste ground called Spitchwick common lying between the river Darte on the west and south east and from thence to Heartor (Yar Tor) to Cornetor (Corndon Tor) on the north and east to the west of Rowbrook hedge and so to Logator (Looka Tor) on the east and so to the river of Darte with free liberty to make a warren there for the keeping breeding and killing of rabbits. And also if any rabbits go over the Darte to the common there called Holne Commons alias Holne Cleyves between Comson (Cumston) hedge and Whortaparke corner or to any place in the said Common of Spitchwicke the said Richard and Walter may kill them. Rent 10/-.*

Vaghill Warren has something approaching thirty 'buries' (to accommodate the rabbits and to encourage their breeding), a feature almost totally absent from Headland Warren. The gulleys of Headland are a good spot to see ring ouzles and, on the high ground around Birch Tor, to see red grouse!

On the north side of the moor, near Sticklepath, lies the site of another

56

warren that erected boundary posts. This is Skaigh Warren, above the river Taw on the north-east side of Cosdon. There are two stones with the letters SZ1/DC1 and SZ2/DC2. These denote a boundary agreement between the commoners of South Zeal and the Duchy of Cornwall, who acquired this warren, later relinquishing it in 1896, when it was referred to as 'Belstone Rabbit Warren'. Eric Hemery in *High Dartmoor* states that one of the stones is known as 'Stumpy Post' – SX 633933.

6

Bridges, Roads and Railways

YET another aspect of boundaries, or 'limits of responsibility', involves County bridges.

Early river crossings were made using clapper bridges and fords. In medieval times, trade in wool and tin became the main source of the county's wealth, and many packhorse bridges were constructed, both by the church, landed-gentry and the county authorities.

Clapper bridges are not now considered to be as old as was once thought. They continued to be built at least until the early nineteenth century, as is shown by the feather-and-tare marks on the stonework of the bridges at Teignhead Farm over the North Teign, and at Lether Tor Farm near Burrator over the Mewy, which is known to date from about 1830. But those bridges on the more important routes over the moor, such as that at Postbridge, generally referred to as the 'Cyclopean Bridge' in older books, probably date from the thirteenth century and later.

The well built packhorse bridges date from the fourteenth century onwards. They are often very graceful structures, high-arched and narrow, with low parapets to accommodate the wide loads carried by strings of packhorses. Many of these older bridges on the edge of the moor, and elsewhere, often still have 'C' stones at each side of their approach, indicating 'County'.

In a statute of Henry VIII, dated 1531, it was stated that unless it could be proved that a 'Hundred, Riding, Wapentake, City, Borough, Town or Parish nor what person certain, or Body Politic should by right Maintain a Bridge', then the shire or county had to maintain them. Thus this 'boundary of responsibility' was indicated by these 'C' stones. These were set at a distance of some hundred yards from the bridge itself, as the county were responsible not only for the fabric of the bridge, but also for the approach, or causeway, the roads at this time being nothing more than mud tracks. One can well imagine the state of the approach to bridges after use by hundreds of packhorses in wet conditions!

Many of these older 'main' roads have now been relegated to secondary status, among them the main Exeter to Plymouth road. On this road, at Harbourneford, there remains a very fine clapper bridge, only about four feet wide. It was for use by foot passengers, beside what used to be a ford. The ford would have been used by all riders and wheeled vehicles and was the butt of caustic comment from James Green in 1809 when he made a survey of all the County bridges of Devon as County Surveyor. He commented of this footbridge that it was 'across a ford which is never dangerous for horses and carriages, and it appears very extraordinary that the County, by taking upon themselves the repair of this bridge should support 200 yards of road on one of the most public Turnpikes in the Kingdom'. At least one of it's 'C' stones still remains.

These 'C' stones are more often found on the right hand side of the road as one approaches the bridge, but some are found on the left. For anyone looking for them, and they are sometimes obscured by vegetation, keep a lookout on both sides of the road.

Some examples of stones relating to bridges on and around the moor are as follows:

Ponsworthy Bridge over the West Webburn at SX 702739. Inset in one of the parapets of this bridge is an upright stone bearing the date 1666, the date of an early repair. A much later repair, of 1911, is recorded by the addition of this date to the same stone. In 1664 it was stated that 'Pounsworthy Bridge, in Withycombe, near the foot of the Mor' was in a state of decay and £30 was needed for its repair.

Shipley Bridge over the Avon at SX 681628 – the 'C' stones on this bridge being on the left side as approached.

Merrivale Bridge over the Walkham at SX 550751 – only the west side 'C' stone remains due to the reallignment of the road. The existing stone is on the now disused part of the road.

Holne Bridge over the Dart at SX 730706 – both stones remain.

Huccaby Bridge over the Dart at SX 659729 – both stones remain.

Bellever Bridge over the East Dart at SX 658774 – both stones remain.

Cadover Bridge over the Plym at SX 555647 – only the east side stone remains on the old, now disused, Cornwood road.

Hill Bridge over the Tavy at SX 532803 – both stones remain.

Piall Bridge over the Piall Brook at SX 596604 – both stones remain.

Langham Bridge at SX 608592, taking the water from Blachford – both stones remain.

'C' stone at Ponsworthy Bridge   *Ponsworthy Bridge (SX 702739)*

59

Sheepstor Bridge is also marked as having these stones on the 1890 Ordnance Survey map, prior to the building of the Burrator reservoir. In spite of the flooding of the valley of the Mewy, the parish bounds are still shown on the line of the inundated river through the reservoir.

Many bridges cross rivers and streams which themselves delineate the parish bounds. The bridge at Ivybridge has already been referred to, along with the pillars bearing the names of the parishes concerned, Ermington and Ugborough. Half Bridge has also been mentioned earlier, on the Okehampton—Tavistock road, having one of the angled two-faced parish stones. The bridge at Sticklepath, over the river Taw, has stones marking the boundaries of Sampford Courtenay ('SC') and South Tawton ('ST'). Dunsford in the Teign valley provides a good example, with separate stones denoting the boundaries of Dunsford and Bridford on the parapet of Steps Bridge. The bridges between Chudleigh and Clifford Bridges are also very interesting. Again at Staverton, where we have a very fine seven-arched bridge over the Dart, there are two stones on one of the refuges having the letters 'D' (Dartington) and 'S' (Staverton).

Sometimes the county went to even greater lengths to mark their responsibility by inserting a tablet into the fabric of the bridge, more usually in the parapet. The mid seventeenth century seems to have been a time of overall survey and repair, with the majority of bridges thus provided being of that period.

Bow Bridge at Bickington, over the River Lemon, on the old road through the village (SX 795725), has both of its 'C' stones and a somewhat fragmented tablet set into the downstream side parapet. In good light most of this is legible, and it reads as follows: 'This Bridge/Repared By The/Covmty in/anno 1688/...'. The rest is more difficult but I think reads 'now restored overal..'.

Drakeford Bridge, on the way into Lustleigh from Reddaford Water at SX 789801, also has a very fine tablet reading 'This 168⅟/Bridg Was/Repard/by The/Covnty'. In 1809 James Green, the County Surveyor, stated that this bridge had a single arch to carry an eight foot roadway, and remarked that it should be rebuilt. At this time it was widened on the upstream side by another six feet. The tablet is in the downstream parapet.

Not far from Drakeford Bridge is another, not named on the 1:25000 map, also over the Bovey. This is Wilford Bridge, SX 799798, now sadly only a roadway supported by steel girders but still retaining its stone abutments. This has a somewhat later tablet dated 1750 reading 'This Bridg/Was Repa/Red By The/Covnty'. Below this has been added '1914', somewhat similarly to Ponsworthy, dating a modern repair. Several bridges were repaired during the years 1911–14, and a number of others have dated metal end plates.

Spara Bridge in the Teign valley, and Yeo Bridge, over the Harbourne, are other bridges of the mid seventeenth century, these having tablets stating the actual year of construction – Spara's reads 'New Builded'!

Until relatively recent times road surfaces were usually in a pretty poor

Drakeford Bridge (SX 789801) *Wilford Bridge (SX 799798)*

state of repair. By and large, maintenance was limited to the filling in of pot-holes with rubble. Bridges, too, were often reported as being in urgent need of repair, while parishes entrusted with maintenance could not afford their upkeep in many instances. Parishes could apply to the county or to turnpike trusts for financial assistance, but where this was denied, parishes simply neglected their responsibility.

The road from Two Bridges to Ashburton was completed as late as 1792, a dated tablet on the bridge over the Dart at Badger's Holt bearing the inscription 'County Bridge 1792' on the upstream side. Until this time the old clapper must have sufficed. Records of that year refer to a Holne section in the surveyors report of the Exeter Trust, stating: 'Aug 9th a man to repair the road in the Chast and Breakin Stons on Goallakecoas 2s4d'. [It has not been possible to establish where this is]; and 'Sept 12th a man & hors to drawing stons on the road to Grenan (Grendon?) and a Buoy 1s11d/6d'. Roadstones were graded, and iron rings were used with a diameter of two or four inches through which the stones were supposed to pass.

With the coming of the turnpikes in the mid eighteenth century, road conditions were somewhat improved in general, and on the fringes of the moor there remain a few relics concerning definitions of limits relating to these trusts.

The best known of these is referred to by Crossing; it is the 'Take off' stone on the Okehampton—Tavistock road belonging to the Tavistock Trust (1762). It is to be found at Beardon at SX 521845 – recently damaged but now happily repaired and replaced. It allowed a carter to hitch up an extra horse to pull his load up the hill on his way to Tavistock as far as this point, where he was obliged to unhitch it. The old turnpike road below this point has been realigned.

A second of these Tavistock Trust stones is on the old Callington—Liskeard road, and a third is to be found at Hurdwick on the old Brentor road.

Another, less well known stone, belongs to the Okehampton Trust (1760), denoting the limit of the roadway under this trust. It is referred to by

61

'Take off' stone, Beardon (SX 521845)

Okehampton Trust stone (SX 523853)

E. Masson Phillips in his notes on 'Marked Stones of Interest' in 1943: 'Down Town Cross lanes Turnpike stone. Where the road from Lydford joins the highway. Here there is, or was, a stone inscribed "End of Okehampton Trust".'

The present author is happy to report that it is still there. At risk to life and limb, a search of the hedgebank all around the immediate area of the minor road into Lydford eventually revealed it on the main road about twenty yards towards Okehampton, on the east side, covered in weeds and mud. To stand back to photograph it requires a second party to look out for the traffic! Of about eighteen inches in height, it has a rounded face. Alongside it is another stone, of equal height, inscribed with the letter 'B'. This is not now on a parish bound, but was it once on the bounds of Bridestowe? Crossing does mention changes in the bounds of Lamerton further along this road, but was there a more general alignment of the parish bounds? Or does this 'B' stone have some other significance?

The author has recently found a similar Okehampton Trust stone near Thorndon Cross at SX 532940, to the west of Okehampton on the old Holsworthy road. Unfortunately a few years ago it was broken off at ground level by a lorry reversing into a gateway, but the upper inscribed part remains in one piece. The author tracked it down to the garden of the nearby Railway Cottages, on the old Stratton and Bude line. Surprisingly the stone was relatively thin, having a flat surface rounded at the sides. It originally stood outside the railway gate at the entrance to these cottages, but in 1986 it was re-erected beside the road by Devon County Council. The letter 'N' has its diagonal stroke reversed thus 'И'.

Other 'End of Trust' stones are placed at the termini of the Okehampton Turnpike Trust on the Launceston, Exbourne and Jacobstowe roads out of Okehampton, and another used to be on the Hatherleigh road, all being sited on parish boundaries.

Railway companies also marked their bounds, but the only railway over Dartmoor proper was the Yelverton—Princetown line, axed by Dr Beeching in 1956. This followed an almost identical route to that taken by its

GWR boundary marker on Princetown Green

63

Moretonhampstead and South Devon Railway boundary stone, present location unknown.

'SDR' – South Devon Railway stone in the grounds of Parke House, Bovey Tracey

predecessor, the Plymouth and Dartmoor Tramway, a horse-drawn railroad constructed by Sir Thomas Tyrwhitt, and opened in 1823 for his quarries at Fogginton and Swell Tor, taking the finished stone to Crabtree Wharf. Though the P.O.W. prison at Princetown was by this time empty and disused, the town was established by virtue of the quarry workers and their needs. Thus Tyrwhitt extended the tramway to Princetown itself, beyond the later GWR station and across what is now the green, to the public house now known as 'The Devil's Elbow', formerly the 'Railway Inn'. On the green we find two boundary markers of the usual GWR pattern, cast iron and circular with a diameter of about five inches, projecting only a couple of inches above the turf, and lettered 'Great Western Railway Cos – Boundary 1898'.

The Moretonhampstead and South Devon Railway was formed in 1866, but by 1872 had been incorporated into the general South Devon Railway system. However it was substantial enough to leave its mark, a bound stone comprising the initial letters of the company. However, the present whereabouts of this stone are unknown.

Later boundary stones, dating from the 1872 period of the South Devon Railway, are inscribed 'SDR' only, without 'M &'. These may now be found outside the main door of Parke, the Dartmoor National Park headquarters at Bovey Tracey, having been removed from the track which used to pass through their grounds.

7

Parole and Other Prison Stones

DARTMOOR – mention the name and in the minds of those not resident in the South West the first thought is often that of the prison at Princetown, rather than the moor itself, a 'resting' place for so many hardened criminals in the past, and now accommodating a wider range of less-hardened cases.

The prison was originally constructed to house prisoners of war captured during the Napoleonic Wars with France. Hostilities with France broke out in 1803, and it was the practice to house prisoners taken during the earlier part of these wars in dismasted hulks in the river estuaries. In South Devon, six hulks were moored in the Hamoaze at Plymouth, but by 1805 they had become so overcrowded and the conditions so terrible that alternative accommodation had to be found.

Sir Thomas Tyrwhitt, the 'founder' of Prince's Town (later Princetown), through his efforts to use 'improved' farming methods in the area to encourage the production of grain and root crops from the unyielding moor, saw the advantages in siting a prisoner of war prison here, both in the national interest, and also his own. Secretary to the Prince of Wales, later George IV after whom he had named Prince's Town, and appointed Auditor to the Duchy of Cornwall, Tyrwhitt later became Lord Warden of the Stannaries of Devon & Cornwall, and was ever well placed to influence decisions.

Commenced in 1806, the prison opened in 1809, and by 1812 there were nine thousand prisoners housed there in conditions hardly better than those they had left in the hulks. However, officers enjoyed a somewhat better 'confinement' compared to the conditions endured by the common soldier. Those officers who gave their word that they would not attempt to escape, were allowed to 'live out' on parole. They are known to have been billetted at Ashburton, Moretonhampstead, Tavistock and Okehampton, and there are records of paroled prisoners at Crediton, North Tawton, South Molton and Tiverton.

This whole subject of prisoners of war is a quite fascinating one, contemporary accounts having been written by both French and American (from the War of 1812) prisoners about their experiences. However, whilst the majority of the prisoners were French or American, there were others from a variety of nations including Danes, Spaniards, Dutch, and Malays and Chinese from East India Company ships.

From the diary of one Silvester Treleaven of Moretonhampstead, records are available of the arrival of the first prisoner-officers in Moreton in 1803, when twenty-four from Tavistock stayed the night before passing through. The first to arrive 'on parole' was recorded in January 1807, and many entries record later arrivals, and departures as 'exchanges' were made with British officers.

Parole stone near Ashburton (SX 748714)

Such 'paroled' officers were allowed to travel up to a mile from the town or village in which they were lodged, and surviving relics of this restriction are the milestones erected for this express purpose on the roads leading from Ashburton.

Residences were 'assigned' to each officer who was also given an allowance of 12/6 per week, regardless of any private means that they might have, which was considerable in some cases. The average farm worker only received about nine shillings per week at this time. Officers were also allowed to trade in any business or occupation they desired, and it is known that amongst men billetted at Ashburton were those who taught modern languages, music and dancing.

The official notice sent to inhabitants of towns selected for residence of prisoners of war stated: 'That all such prisoners are permitted to walk or ride, on the great turnpike road within a distance of 1 Mile from the extreme parts of the town (not beyond the bounds of the Parish), and that if they shall exceed such limits or go into any field or Cross-road they may be taken up and sent to prison and a reward of 10/- will be paid by the agent for apprehending them'.

In the case of Ashburton, no less than seven such parole stones are known to have been erected on roads out of the town. Those found by the author are simply inscribed '1/Mile', without any other direction, and stand on the Broadhempston road up Whistley Hill (SX 768690), and on Druid's Hill just below the entrance to the mine captain's cottage (SX 748714). A stone on the Woodland road is said to have been purposely hidden with turf by the farmer

66

at Dipwell to discourage souvenir hunters! Another was on the Buckland road between Water Turn and Highgrove but the author has failed to find this. Old six inch maps also show stones at one mile from the town at SX 740699 on the Holne road and at Alston Cross on the old A38, now bypassed by the newer dual carriageway. The stone on Druid's Hill measured a mile from Great Bridge, the 'extreme' of the town at that time.

It is also said that the stone on the Broadhempston road, which incidentally, appears on the Ordnance Survey 1:25 000 map though not a milestone in the proper sense of the word, was moved by the prisoners 'so as to allow them to see round the next bend'. Examination of this stone at it's present site shows it to be in the middle of a straight stretch of road! A reference to Tavistock in this respect records the comment of an old inhabitant, that the prisoners 'were artful in moving the Milestones and Borough Bounds'. In Moretonhampstead it seems that the milestones of the 1772 Turnpike were generally accepted as markers for the parole limit.

On the road leading out of Widecombe towards Natsworthy there is a curious stone inscribed 'I miol' – an instance of a phonetic spelling in the broad Devon accent. Though there appears to be no record of Widecombe as a parole town, it seems quite likely that this is what the stone was intended for. A Lt Col. Hughes, writing in the *Transactions of the Devonshire Association* (1954) referred to 'Many (parole) towns', implying that there were more than the eight referred to above.

Finally a special dispensation was given to those officers quartered at Princetown. William Crossing's *Ancient Crosses of Dartmoor*, written in 1887, refers to Ollsbrim Cross, now reinstated in its rightful place at the junction of the Tavistock—Ashburton and Widecombe roads (SX 685735), on the Church Way to Widecombe. Crossing writes:

Parole stone Widecombe to Natsworthy road (SX 721779)

Mr Dymond informs me that, on the authority of old William French, of the Higher Lodge, Spitchwick, who has spent all his life there, that this cross, when standing in it's place on the moor (removed at that time to a farm at Leusdon and used as a gate post) was fixed upon as the limit to which French Prisoners of War Officers detained at Princetown, at the commencement of this century were permitted to extend their walks on parole of honour.

This cross is in excess of seven miles from the prison!

The main bulk of prisoners had left the prison by 1815, and the sick ones by 1816. Thereafter the prison remained empty until pressed into use for criminals in 1850, and has continued to be so used ever since.

There are two boundary markers on the line of the Forest bounds which relate to the first acquisition of land by the prison authorities, to the north and to the south of North Hessary Tor. Both of these stones are made of the local, very coarse red granite and bear a large six-inch arrow. They are sited along with other plain Forest bound stones erected at a later date, re-aligning the Forest bounds between North Hessary and Mistor.

Also associated with the prison are a number of smaller granite boundary stones no more than eighteen inches high, square of shaft, and with a peaked

Ollsbrim Cross (SX 685735)

68

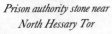

Prison authority stone near
North Hessary Tor

Directors of Convict Prison' stone,
Princetown

top, bearing the inscription 'DCP/↑'. They are found by the roadside from Two Bridges to Princetown, and also Two Bridges to Holming Beam, and around the Holming Beam land including the track to Mistor.

The author has previously assumed that the letters 'DCP' referred to 'Dartmoor Convict Prison' (or 'Criminal Prison'), but through recent correspondence with a prison officer this assumption has to be revised. The prison has several old maps of the area showing 'Land held on Lease by the Directors of Convict Prisons', and that drawings bore a rubber stamp mark reading 'Directors of Convict Prisons'. It thus seems pretty conclusive that the boundary stone letters would refer to the same authority. The Directors of Convict Prisons later became simply 'The Prison Commisioners', the current title being 'Home Office Prisons'.

Also within prison property, to the south-east of Mistor, are five other boundstones, shown on the Ordnance Survey six inch maps. These surround a source of the prison's water supply.

8

The Stone Cutters

DARTMOOR granite has been used by man ever since he first visited the moor, as the vast amount of Bronze Age remains testify. This surface stone, the shattered and scattered, remains of tors is referred to as 'moorstone', and was used almost exclusively in building dwellings and farm enclosures. Stone cutting was done by means of a series of cuts or slots into which wedges were hammered until it split.

The construction of the prison at Princetown in 1806–09, at the instigation of Sir Thomas Tyrwhitt, from moorstone on Walkhampton Common, realised the full potential of this stone. Shortly after 1800 an easier method of splitting the stone was introduced, the 'feather-and-tare', and early in the 1820s Tyrwhitt leased land from the Duchy and opened quarries at Foggintor. With the opening of his Plymouth and Dartmoor tramway in 1823 he was able to carry the cut stone down to Crabtree Wharf in Plymouth for shipment. At that time the line only went as far as the quarries of Swell Tor and Foggintor; it was not until later that he extended it to Princetown.

Under Foggintor and King Tor outside the Yellowmeade Farm enclosures are four plain granite boundary posts. They bear the mark of the feather-and-tare and thus date later than about 1803. Yellowmeade Farm itself was not established until 1860, the last farm to be founded in Walkhampton Parish. There are still the remains of workers cottages at Foggintor on the rubble heap, where the author's wife lived for a short while in the late 1920s and early '30s, known as Hill Cottages. Alongside the 'Yellowmeade' track, largely the bed of what was once one of the quarry tramways, near the quarry, are some part-finished stones made by members of her family, a number of whom were stone-masons. These were made after the Foggintor quarry closed. The cottages at Foggintor get little mention in various publications about the moor, though there are several references to Red Cottages, now completely demolished, at West View, nearer the main road. It is interesting to note that the Census Return for 1866 recorded no less than 267 persons living in the Foggintor and Rundlestone area.

About the time Tyrwhitt was opening up Foggintor, George Templer was opening the Haytor quarries, transporting his stone via a granite tramway, an unusual innovation, to Ventiford at the head of the Stover Canal which his father had constructed in the 1790s for his ball clay business in the Bovey Basin. Using barges the stone was then taken to Teignmouth from where it was shipped. The trans-shipment by barge was an extra operation avoided by other producers of building stone, and is one of the reasons for Templer's failure. Native granite was used for the tramway rails, with a flange on the inside of the rail. Gravity alone took the trucks down to sea-level from a height of some 1450 feet. In Britain there appears to be only one other use of stone rails, this on an inclined plane in Yorkshire limestone country where the flange on the rail was on the outside. Tyrwhitt made some use of granite in the 'sidings' of his quarry tramway.

Templer marked off the miles on his tramway with milestones, numbers 3 to 6 of which remain in situ. The author has discovered one solitary boundary stone north-east of the main quarry and to the north of the tramway at approx. SX 763779. This is a well-shaped stone with a domed top, having a carefully incised 'T' on the west face and a much cruder 'S' on the reverse side, the Duke of Somerset's mark.*

'Shewte Rights' stone, near Yarner Nature Reserve

* By 1829 George Templer was in financial difficulties and sold the Haytor quarries and Stover Canal to the Duke of Somerset, together with his residence at Stover.

Following the track of Templer's granite tramway one day the author discovered another boundary stone lettered 'Shewte Rights', one of two stones, the other being blank. These are on the bridlepath from Reddaford Water to the Haytor—Bovey road. Enquiring of the owner of Shewte, the author was favoured with the following reply:

> *It was originally marked as our grazing rights on what was once common land before it was enclosed, and, we believe, squatted on many years ago. It would be in that position because just recently we have pulled down a stone shed on the farm and have found that marker stones, or granite posts, were buried underneath and in one case used to make a step – and on one of these is written 'Lower Down of Yarner Down'. Once upon a time the whole will have been referred to as Yarner Down, and then the piece below the railway as 'Lower Down'. It was just rough grazing when we first came here. This farm was once part of the Yarner Estate and when it was split up some of the rights were sold off separately.*

Another 'Yarner' marked stone still exists beside the road at the junction of the parishes of Bovey Tracey and Lustleigh on Trendlebere Down, a rough set stone marked with the letter 'Y' at SX 779793.

On the western side of the moor also, there were extensively quarried areas, in particular Whitchurch Common, where the mark of the feather-and-tare is everywhere. Pu Tor, Heckwood Tor and Feather Tor were

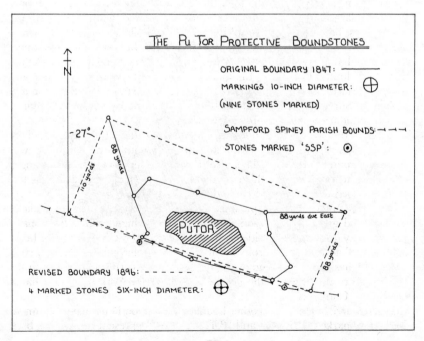

THE PU TOR PROTECTIVE BOUNDSTONES

ORIGINAL BOUNDARY 1847: ———

MARKINGS 10-INCH DIAMETER: ⊕

(NINE STONES MARKED)

SAMPFORD SPINEY PARISH BOUNDS: –⊣–⊣–⊣

STONES MARKED 'SSP': ⊙

N

-27°

110 yards

88 yards

88 yards due East

88 yards

PU TOR

REVISED BOUNDARY 1896: - - - - - -

4 MARKED STONES SIX-INCH DIAMETER: ⊕

particularly affected, together with the slopes of the Staple Tors where so many set-makers benches remain – these the origin of so many of the cobbled roads of the mid-nineteenth century.

Leases giving the right to cut stone were obtained from the Duchy of Cornwall from the 1840s, for a fuller account of which readers should refer to an article in the *Transactions of the Devonshire Association* (1981), by Helen Harris. Such was the demand for stone, and damaging encroachment on the tors themselves, that in 1847 limits were set around Pu Tor within which it was forbidden to remove stone. All contractors to whom leases were made were obliged to conform to these limits.

The full significance of the marked stones around Pu Tor was not fully appreciated until Helen Harris published her paper. In the 1847 series there were nine natural boulders around the tor which were marked with an incised device like a hot-cross bun so: $\oplus$. These marks had a diameter of ten inches.

When Mr Duke of Merrivale Quarry, which opened in 1876, needed to renew his licence in 1896, the Duchy offered him a fresh grant showing even more extended protective limits around the tor, with an agreement that 'Mr Duke would have marks cut in blocks of stone to define the limits'. On the 30 December 1896 it was reported that 'Mr Duke has had marks cut in some natural stones to indicate the New Protective Limits of Pu Tor, each mark being a circle with five holes about an inch deep to distinguish them from the original marks by a cross within a circle.'

Whereas the old bound had been close up to the tor, and of a ten sided shape, the new bound of 1896 took the form of a rough rectangle with only four boundary markers, and these smaller and more difficult to see than the earlier ones, having a diameter of but six inches. When Helen Harris wrote her paper, two of these four stones had been found, but only one cannot now be traced, that at the north-east corner. The last stone to be found was at the north-west limit and this has the marking both on its horizontal surface and its vertical face, near the old quarry. None of these stones is marked on any Ordnance Survey maps, but along the southern line two Sampford Spiney Parish boundary stones are only a few yards distant.

At about the same period, not far away to the north, on the other side of the Two Bridges to Tavistock road, a somewhat similar arrangement was enforced around Roos Tor. This also included a series of stones defining a limit to protect that tor. In this case there are thirteen stones around the tor, each inscribed with a divided circle thus: $\ominus$

These are not all that conspicuous, and to emphasise the limit the Duke of Bedford had granite pillars some four or five feet high erected fractionally further away from the tor beside each of these natural rocks. Each pillar bears the letter 'B' and they date from about 1880. It is believed that the Duke was laying emphasis on the bound as the result of much correspondence with the Duchy before the grant of the licence was made for work here, on what is Peter Tavy Common.

Helen Harris refers to two other boundary stones on Peter Tavy Common. These are marked 'P.T.G.1' and 'P.T.G.2' but the present author has been

One of the Duke of Bedford stones around Roos Tor

unable to trace them. Helen Harris writes: 'On Nov 1st 1847 a licence to quarry granite within a portion of the Commons of Devon north and south of the road leading from Tavistock to Merrivale Bridge was granted by the Prince of Wales (Duke of Cornwall) to two Tavistock men, Joseph Edgcumbe, a chemist and druggist, and John White, a wine and spirit merchant. The northern boundary of the area was defined as 'a straight line from a post marked P.T.G.1 placed by the boundary of the Commons at or near Wedlake (Peter Tavy) to a stone post marked P.T.G.2 on the west bank of the River Walkham at or near Hanging Rock'. In the Ordnance Survey Boundary Report Books, Hanging Rock is shown much further down the Walkham than Deadlake, where the author had supposed it to be. In fact it is shown at SX 556777, almost on the same latitude as the northern extremity of the Wedlake enclosures. No sign of P.T.G.2 has been found despite a thorough search.

9

The Army

THE army have trained on Dartmoor for many years, reference having been made to manoeuvres on Roborough Down as early as 1794. An encampment was set up on Hemerdon Ball at about the same time, both of these activities no doubt training exercises during a period when we were under threat of invasion from Napoleon – the French and Spanish fleets actually being sighted off Plymouth in 1779.

In 1873 manoeuvres were held on several areas of the moor under canvas – they even had Field Post Offices with the numbers G17 and G18 allocated to them, desirable items for the postal historian. From 1884 camps were sited on the slopes of Haytor and Saddle Tor, of which photographic postcards survive. All these camps were of a temporary nature.

There are existing signs of military activity of yesteryear, even from the era of smooth-bore barrels. Under Yes Tor on Longstone Hill the author has found (walkers are reminded not to pick up metal objects!) many pieces of musket shot, lead balls of some 14mm diameter mostly, but a few of even larger size. Some of these are mis-shapen, but others are perfect, showing the join of the hand-cast mould round the diameter, and also where each bullet was joined to the next (the moulds usually casting four of these 14mm balls at one time, the molten metal being poured into one end of a hinged contraption somewhat like a pair of tongs).

These musket balls have been brought to the surface again by vehicles of the present day army. The author has variously been advised that these bullets date from the sixteenth to nineteenth century, more specifically from the eighteenth and nineteenth century. Being in some profusion at this particular spot, not so far from Sourton Down where the Royalists and Roundheads had their skirmish in April 1643, with the Royalists under Sir Ralph Hopton, and the Parliamentarians under General James Chudleigh, is it possible they result from this affray? It is recorded that the Parliamentarians routed the Royalists at their first attempt, and disrupted the entire army. A violent thunderstorm made the Royalists retreat to Bridestowe and the following morning Chudleigh collected almost a thousand muskets and pikes, five barrels of powder and other equipment left by the fleeing Royalists. But in truth these bullets are probably of early Victorian origin! Eric Hemery in *High Dartmoor* gives the name 'Snipers Gully Stream' to a left bank tributary of the Redaven nearby – perhaps this gives a clue to the origin of the musket balls.

But to boundary stones: the army now have ranges at Okehampton, Merrivale and Willsworthy, and at the latter they purchased their first tract of land, virtually following the line of the old Willsworthy Manor, in about

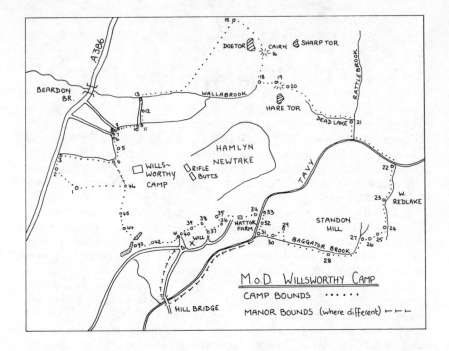

M.o.D. WILLSWORTHY CAMP
CAMP BOUNDS ......
MANOR BOUNDS (where different) ⊢⊢⊢

1900. These bounds are marked by no less than forty-six granite posts, about two and a half feet in height, bearing the letters 'WD' and a number, ranging from 1 to 46, as shown on the accompanying map.

The position of these boundary stones is as follows:

1 SX 518826 – on Black Hill
2 SX 5175832 – Okehampton—Tavistock roadside
3 SX 518835 – Willsworthy Gate
4 SX 522834 – Prescombe Corner
5 SX 522836 – Sounscombe Head
6 SX 521837 – (between)
7 SX 520838 – Sounscombe Foot
8 SX 521839 – Beardon Gate
9 SX 521839 – Beardon Gate
10 SX 524841 – Lissicombe Head
11 SX 524841 – Lissicombe Head
12 SX 524843 – (between)
13 SX 523844 – Lissicombe Foot
14 SX (not identified) – Wallabrook
15 SX541849 – Doe Tor Bottom near Tavistock water intake
16 SX544849 – cist east of Doe Tor
17 SX (not identified)

76

18 SX 544845 – Wallabrook Head
19 SX 551845 – cairn north Hare Tor – manor Hey Tor boundstone
20 SX 555846 – Deadlake Head
21 SX 561840 – Deadlake Foot, Tavy to
22 SX 566832 – Western Redlake Foot
23 SX 565828 – half way up the Western Redlake
24 SX 565825 – near Western Redlake Head
25 SX 565818 – near Baggator Brook head
26 SX 564816 – ditto
27 SX 562814 – ditto
28 SX 555808 – NW South Common plantation
29 SX 549811 – NW corner Baggator Woods
30 SX 548899 – SW Corner Baggator Woods
31 SX 540811 – Cataloo Steps on Tavy
32 SX 539815 – Standon Steps on Tavy
33 SX 546820 – on Tavy left bank
34 SX 544820 – on Tavy right bank
35 SX 531822 ⎱
36 SX 531821 ⎰ bordering and taking in the old Yellowmeade enclosures
37 SX 531821 – taking in the old Yellowmeade enclosures
38 SX 530822 – ditto
39 SX 529822 – ditto
40 SX 529816 – Buddla Corner
41 SX 529816 – Buddla Corner
42 SX 527815 – (between)
43 SX 525813 – (between)
44 SX 526819 – Down Pool
45 SX 524822 – Tin Pits
46 SX 523825 – crest of Black Hill

One of the many War Department stones around Willsworthy

10

China Clay Country

MILLIONS of years ago in the Bovey Basin a large amount of ball clay was deposited by waters draining from the granite masses on Dartmoor. However, in the south west, principally on Lee Moor and those other moors in the immediate vicinity, the granite has not been redeposited by water action, rather it has lain rotting, the feldspar crystals becoming a fine clay. This china clay is extracted by hosing it out at pressure into a suspended solution. The huge waste tips we now see are the 90 per cent waste matter of quartz and mica.

Lord Morley first leased land in this area in 1830 for the exploitation of the china clay, and in 1833 William Phillips further developed this undertaking, being joined by his son in 1835 or 1836. The Phillips leat now dry, took water off the Lannacombe for washing purposes. The old Bottle Hill Mine leat is still used for the same purpose emptying into Big Pond.

Perhaps some of the best views of these workings are to be had from Penn Beacon and Shell Top, looking down from the east side. They can be approached from Cadworthy Bridge and Trowlesworthy, Shell Top being the central point. Shell Top itself has been used as a boundary mark. It bears an incised cross on a vertical face, and also a triangular device with a hole in the centre on the top face for a flag pole, used for wartime army field firing exercises. This is lettered AR/WR.

South-west of Shell Top are three massive stones marking the boundaries of Penn Moor and Lee Moor and lettered 'PM' and 'LM' on their respective sides. They are all at least six feet in height and the Ordnance Survey show two on their 1:25 000 scale maps where they mark the parish bounds of Cornwood and Shaugh Prior. These two are at SX 593634 and SX 591632.

The third stone, nearer Shell Top, above a very fine Bronze Age settlement site at SX 595636, is now fallen – probably the reason why the Ordnance Survey omit it from their map.

The other boundary running down from Shell Top is that dividing Lee Moor from Shaugh Moor. It follows the Blackabrook to a point at SX 576638 where an old gate post, complete with holes for two gate hangers, has been utilized as a boundary stone above the right bank, almost at the southern end of a stone row. The line now follows the brook for about half a mile. Where the boundary leaves the brook is another boundary stone, this on the left bank, lettered 'LM/1835' and 'SM/1835', dated at just the time Phillips and his son were developing the clay industry.

There is a more obvious and similarly lettered stone, albeit much better fashioned and bearing the marks of the feather-and-tare, beside the Cadover or Cadworthy to Cornwood road, now disused except by the Lee Moor

Penn Moor—Lee Moor bound
stone (SX 593634)

Lee Moor bound stone on the
Blackabrook

workers (SX 569634). The line continues to Emmet's Post, sited on the remains of a cairn at SX 567632, bearing the letters 'LM' and 'SM'.

Whilst Lord Morley owned Lee Moor and leased land to Phillips and, later, others, Shaugh Moor belonged to the Lopes family. William Crossing, in his reference to the inscriptions on Emmet's Post, gets himself into a bit of a tangle, giving the inscription both incomplete and face-about!

Even the latest Outdoor Leisure Map is out of date so far as the clay workings go. On a recent search for a couple of other stones marked on the old six inch maps, and which the author suspected continued this Lee Moor—Shaugh Moor boundary line south-east of Saddleborough on Shaugh Moor, there were lorries depositing loads of waste material and the moor was covered.

Not so far distant from the Saddleborough area is Wotter, above which there are two stones bearing the letter 'H'. Hemery states that he could find no connection with these and Hemerdon House but the present author is not so sure as there is another stone thus marked much nearer to Hemerdon on Smallhanger Waste. One of the stones referred to by Hemery is near Collard Tor. It is a rough-set stone on the line of an ancient field wall at SX 558622. The other is nearer Hawks Tor where army anti-aircraft guns or searchlights were positioned during the second world war (SX 551622).

Hawks Tor itself is a most interesting phenomenon, and has been written about at least since the close of the eighteenth century. A full record of the relative position of the capstone over the curious 'shelter' is detailed by Richard Hansford Worth in the *Transactions of the Devonshire Association* (1941), where he expounds the opinion that the shelter it is indeed man-made and not natural. To those unaware of the special feature of this tor, it has not unusually got a quartz fault running through it. What is interesting is that this vein in the capstone, or upper layer of what used to be the tor, lies at almost a ninety degree angle to the vein in the rest of the tor. It is difficult to see the justification for the energy and ingenuity that must have been expended to form what is only a very rough shelter for a few sheep, one side of the capstone being supported as it is by a loose rock. Not only this, but an attempt has been made to cut the capstone using the old cold-chisel method, thus dating it prior to 1800. To view the whole is to wonder at the force that must have been necessary to move it, if indeed it was done by man.

Somewhat further south are a number of other workings, many abandoned, at Headon. If we take a walk from Tolchmoor Gate (SX 581616) to the old, now abandoned farm at Broomage, we come to Crownhill Down. Under Crownhill Tor, from the stile, we can see not one but two dry leats, pot leats to Broomage and Mumford Cottage. By proceeding farther down towards the Torycombe Valley we will come across yet another dry leat. This is the old Bottle Hill Mine leat. Bottle Hill Mine, opened in 1715, produced some tin, considerable copper, and some mispickel and arsenic. The mine chimney is still a familiar landmark.

Just below this dry leat, which can be followed for about a mile, are a series of boundary markers, seven in number, each inscribed 'LM/1887', obviously a boundary extension for china clay workings. These stones extend from SX 569606 to 577612. There is another unmarked stone of the same period at SX 576608, and several others further south on Crownhill Down.

Earlier in this chapter reference is made to a third 'H' stone near Hemerdon House. This lies between old unworked pits at SX 578595. It has an 'H' on the west face and 'V' on the east face. There is no clue to the source to the letter 'V'! North-west of this stone are the remains of earlier workings, including two large settling pits somewhat similar to those at Shipley Bridge, though not lined, and a series of mica settling channels. Hemerdon Mine is nearby, too, about to be re-opened for the production of tungsten.

In this vicinity the author discovered yet another stone, not a boundstone, but nevertheless interesting. North of Sparkwell near the Hemerdon entrance, at SX 576586 it reads: H.H.T/1862/The/Sea . Level/of . this/Place . is/682.Feet.

At a little distance from the china clay centre is Wigford Down, another site of boundary markers. Approached by way of Cadover Bridge itself, or from the northern side south of Durance Farm, Wigford Down has, like many other areas on the moor, a wealth of Bronze Age remains: many reaves (not marked on the 1:25 000 scale maps), cairns and hut circles. There is a very fine cist which also is not marked on the map.

The appropriate Outdoor Leisure map shows a diagonal green line running across the down north-west to south-east. This is the bound of the National Trust land centred around Goodameavy, and encompassing the Dewerstone and the Dewerstone quarries. Along this line are no less than six

'H.H.T.' – a possible connection with Hemerdon House? (SX 576586)

boundary stones. These are set stones of nineteenth century date, since they show signs of feather-and-tare. They follow the line of older natural stones or, nearer the crest of the down, an old reave. About four and a half feet tall, they all bear the letter 'L'. The six inch Ordnance Survey map shows only two of these, and the National Trust brochure five, missing just one.

There is a seventh stone beside the road near Higher Beliver Farm on the Hoo Meavy road. The author's first thought was that the letter 'L' represented Lovaton Farm, quite nearby, but Brian le Messurier believed that they belong to the Lopes family. Following the line to the summit of the down and just beyond, towards the enclosures of Lower Cadworthy Farm, near the corner, will be found the cist at SX 544644. To the south west is the Dewerstone with its collection of carved inscriptions to the poet Carrington, and others, and the remains of the Iron Age fort.

The Bronze Age reaves include a number to the south of Durance, and some of the present walls are built upon them. At the southernmost point of these enclosures, near the cairn at the height of the down, is a single small eighteen inch high boundary marker inscribed 'BA', the letter 'A' being particularly individually shaped.

If any reader knows its purpose the author would be pleased to have details. It appears to mark the outer bound of what are now enclosed fields, built on reaves, and it has been suggested by Eric Hemery in *High Dartmoor*

Unidentified stone at SX 548651,
near Durance

John Scoble's stone near
Dewerstone Cottages

that the inscription might refer to either Brisworthy Arrishes or the Domesday manor 'Bachemora'. R. G. Haynes suggests the reference is to Buckland Abbey.

Urgles Cross is a complete modern replacement and does not appear on the Ordnance Survey map. It stands on the green opposite Urgles Cottages on the south side of the road, on the site of an ancient socket stone. However, modern as the cross may be, it is nicely proportioned and pleasing to the eye. Further down this road, near the bridge over the Meavy, is a stone in a wall on the south side that has always intrigued the author. An oblong block some eighteen inches or so long, it bears the inscription 'JS/1832', and is adjacent to the entrance to Dewerstone Cottages. It is known that the initials refer to one J. Scoble, a former landowner, but for what purpose? The land is now part of the National Trust holding.

Enter the path to the cottages and within a few hundred yards there is an unfinished tramway embankment, complete with a tunnel. This track, from the Dewerstone Quarry, was intended to link up with the South Devon line to Yelverton, but permission was not granted by the owner of the small stretch of land west of the river, quite possibly Lopes. It is extraordinary to consider the amount of work that went into building the tramway, on a considerable embankment, and with one complete tunnel and another partially built, without permission first being sought from all the landowners concerned – or was an agreement revoked at the last minute?

11

Water Undertakings

THE rainfall over Dartmoor is prodigious and many of Devon's rivers rise in the blanket bogs of Dartmoor's granite mass, their waters having been utilized by all manner of industry. In the early days of tin 'streaming', in medieval times, the courses of rivers were diverted to wash through the workings. Later the water-wheel was introduced to provide power to crush ore with 'stamps', and to provide power for bellows to fan the charcoal to a sufficient temperature to smelt the ore. Water power was also enslaved to pump out later workings where shafts and levels became flooded.

Many other industries, principally the host of corn and woollen mills situated in the 'in country' and below, also relied on water for their power. Leats were dug to channel these waters to provide a sufficient 'head' of water to propel the water-wheels, some leats having to run for a considerable distance. Rights to water were jealously guarded but pot-water leats were allowed to draw off from major leats with a limit to the amount of water taken. In order that the users in the lower course of the leat were not deprived of water, pot-water leats obtained their water by means of what is known as a 'bull's eye' stone. This slab of stone was drilled with a hole an inch in diameter. The stone was fixed into the bank of the leat on the 'lower' side, ensuring that the greater volume of water passed further down.

There are several 'bull's eyes' taking water off the Grimstone and Sortridge Leat, which originates from the right bank of the Walkham river above the three blowing houses near Merrivale. There is one at Windy Post, the guide cross on the old Tavistock–Ashburton track at SX 533743, and another only a few yards away giving water to Moortown Farm. Lower still under Pu Tor 'bulls eyes' take water for Langstone, Oakley, etc. Two more are on the Holne Moor leat, taking water to Seale's Stoke Farm at SX 694709, and Middle Stoke Farm, SX 697705. These are interesting in that to ensure that rights to a water supply were not impaired, the leat was piped under Venford Reservoir which was built in the years 1905–7. West Stoke Farm, nearby, did not get its water from that source, but from the Holne Town Leat or Gutter, taking water off below the old Ringleshutes Mine. Here, in addition to the concrete 'bull's eye' in use, is another granite one set aside on the bank. It would appear that the old granite one often became choked with weed as the newer one has a metal grid fixed to it to get over that problem.

The first major leat taking water for human consumption was Drake's Leat built in the sixteenth century. This took water from the Meavy or Mewy at a point now under the Burrator Reservoir, and supplied Devonport and the ships victualled there. A dry granite-lined section can still be seen running

Burrator Reservoir stone at head mire of the Meavy

from the foot of the dam to the Meavy road, and it is only recently that the arched tunnel of the leat was found underground in Plymouth when building excavations were being made.

Drake's Leat was followed by the Devonport Leat, constructed in 1793, when the earlier leat proved inadequate. This still draws water from the Cowsic and West Dart rivers, some emptying into the reservoir to supplement the rest of the water from the catchment area.

Burrator Reservoir was built across the river Meavy by the Plymouth Corporation Water Works and opened in September 1898. Land has been purchased so that waters draining into the Meavy above the dam were all captured, and the bounds of this land is now marked by a number of boundary stones. These were not erected until between 1917 and 1932. All are dated and inscribed with the initials 'PCWW', all this land now being held by the South West Water Authority.

The land purchased ran from below the northern side of the dam, over Yennadon Down, crossed the Yelverton to Princetown road just below the Goadstone pool on the divide, and passing under Leedon Tor, crossed Walkhampton Common to North Hessary Tor, across the Walkham–Meavy divide. The boundary stones are mostly dated 1917, but at North Hessary the tor itself was inscribed on its western face. The line then ran to South Hessary Tor, recrossing the road just on the outskirts of Princetown by the lodges erected by Tyrwhitt. These boundary markers are also dated 1917. However, between North Hessary and the road there are three boundary stones dated as late as 1932, these taking in the head mire of the Meavy on land that had been within the Forest bounds.

From South Hessary the boundary followed the same line as the Forest to Eylesbarrow, where it turned westward to follow a parallel path to the old miners' track, passing to the east of Yellowmead Farm and Four Fold Circle, and up and over Sheepstor's lofty crest. These latter stones are dated 1919.

Similarly, Venford Reservoir, opened in 1907 and supplying water to Paignton, has a series of boundary markers defining the land purchased by Paignton Urban District Council from the then Lord of the Manor of Holne. The initials of the Lord of the Manor, Richard Dawson are inscribed on one side of each marker, 'RD/H', and Paignton's initials, 'PUDC' on the other. This land, though small in extent, does border the Sandy Way and reaches almost to the northern slope of Ryder's Hill. The stone on the divide between the O Brook and the Venford Brook bears the arrow of the surveyors – a bench mark. A photograph of the dam under construction in 1905 shows the old bridge over the Venford Brook – perhaps it is still standing under the water, though it never appears at times of drought as does the bridge at Fernworthy Reservoir.

From 1934 the natural waters draining into this small reservoir at Venford were found to be insufficient for Paignton's needs, and since that date water has been pumped from the Swincombe to augment supplies.

Vennford Reservoir stone, inscribed with Richard Dawson's initials

85

There are now paths around this reservoir. Just by the western entrance there is the triple stamp mortar stone, referred to by Eric Hemery in *High Dartmoor*, which used to be beside the water foreman's house. The whole valley, as with similar valleys on the moor, has been extensively worked for tin, and it is probable that the blowing house was situated more or less where the dam stands today. The sunken approach to both sides of the old bridge is clearly visible, which the photograph shows as being similar to Saddle Bridge.*

However these reservoirs were not by any means the first to take water from the granite country. Negotiations for Tottiford reservoir, near Hennock, were started as early as 1856, and it started to supply Torquay with water in 1858, a full forty years before Burrator was completed. As a stamp collector, the author has recently sold a letter/entire dated December 1855 headed 'Tormohun Waterworks' (Construction of Waterworks) whereby a party 'assents' to the proposal. This complex now includes Kennick and Trenchford, and has pleasant level walks around them.

Another very small enclosure from which water was extracted for the town of Tavistock is to be found on the Doetor Brook at SX 541851. Here above the right bank there are two markers lettered 'TRDC'. Close by on the opposite bank is the Willsworthy War Department stone numbered '15', as stated in Chapter 9, one of forty-six numbered markers.

*The author's wife has the photographs of this bridge. They have been used to illustrate *A Dartmoor Century – 1883–1983* published by the Dartmoor Preservation Association on the occasion of their centenary (page 45), and show work starting on the dam in the background. Another photograph, taken at the same time but not shown in the centenary book, depicts a crane or sheerlegs at work. Dr Tom Greeves, who wrote up all the photographs, dated these as 'in about 1903', although the dam was actually started in 1905.

12

Miscellaneous Boundary Stones

THE stones included in this chapter either do not fit in with any of the categories previously described or are or an unknown origin to the author.

The Rattlebrook Peat Works
This concern worked from the mid nineteenth century until about 1930. The peat was worked both for fuel, when it was compressed into blocks, and also for the production of naptha, similar to the Shipley Bridge works. Latterly a narrow-gauge railway ran from the Rattlebrook Head to Bridestowe where it connected with the main line. The ruins of Bleak House is the place more often visited today for the letter box – this was the works manager's house.

The first Duchy records date from 1868, and in 1878 the West of England Compressed Peat Company Limited were granted a lease to work an area of one square mile (see Helen Harris, *Industrial Archaeology of Dartmoor* for further details).

There is one boundary stone at SX 566833 where the Western Redlake meets the Tavy. Another plain pillar is to be found on the south-east side of Great Links Tor, a Duchy stone, probably of the 1880s.

Neither Bridestowe or Sourton have a boundary on the Forest, but the two parishes jointly have lands which do, thus producing boundary stones lettered 'BSL', Bridestowe and Sourton Lands.

'CW2' – a Mystery Stone
Just outside the old enclosures of the fourteenth century farm known as Huckentor Farm, near Little King Tor, there is on the open moor a four and a half feet high granite pillar so inscribed. Criptor Waste has been suggested, but the author is very doubtful of this explanation. He would be pleased to hear from anyone with definite information.

'RB' Stones
On the 1:25 000 Ordnance Survey maps between Collaton Lane and the Boundary Rock at Beckamoor Head, and parallel with the road at Pork Hill, there are 'B.S.', severally marked between SX 524 to 527/754, on the Peter Tavy and Whitchurch parish bounds.

These turn out to be very rough-set stones, only a foot or eighteen inches high, six in number and all marked 'RB', or the lower part of those letters, as some have been broken off at the top.

William Crossing in *One Hundred Years on Dartmoor*, relates the story about the introduction of wheeled vehicles to Dartmoor and of a farmer in Peter Tavy Parish, the first to have a cart to collect peat from the ties. The farmer

'RB' stones on the Peter Tavy—Whitchurch parish bounds

concerned was, he believed, one William Reep of Coxtor Farm. Also Eric Hemery in *High Dartmoor* in a footnote states that Little Cox Tor was spoken of as 'Reep's Tor', since the Reep family ran sheep up there at the end of the last century.

The bound stones would appear to be of earlier date but the Reep family are known to have farmed on Dartmoor since the fourteenth century. Perhaps the 'RB' stones refer to an earlier generation?

Mary Tavy – Hilnor or Hope Mine
On the verge outside the house known as 'Hilnor' on the Brentor road out of Mary Tavy there is a stone with the inscription 'HB/ 1'. At Downland Farm on the eastern side of the main road there is another from the same series lettered 'HB/5', this now acting as a step to the gate at the front entrance. Obviously, there were, or are, others. Is it a coincidence that No 1 is outside Hilnor? Or might they refer to Hope Mine?

Assycombe Hill – Asacombe Hill
At the crest of the hill just outside the Fernworthy Forest, and the wall enclosing same at SX 665820, there is a boundary stone bearing the single letter 'D', not easy to see except in a favourable light. This is believed to relate to the Duchy, though it stands within the Forest Bounds. It is sited on the scant remains of a cairn.

'HB' stone near Hilnor

Dartmoor Preservation Association
stone at Sharpitor

In conclusion, though the markings of bounds was an ancient process it still continues today, with an additional boundary stone erected here and there to emphasise a point. As has been stated the parish bounds are now being beaten more regularly, by and large, and more interest taken in them. That erected by Lustleigh on the by-road to Chagford at SX 749847 a few years ago has even been dated.

Also in recent times the Dartmoor Preservation Association itself had a series of five boundary markers erected around Sharpitor, marking the thirty-two acres purchased from the South West Water Authority with funds from the Sylvia Sayer Fund. These markers, some two feet high and with a rounded top, have an oval sunken panel which has the letters 'DPA' inscribed on it. Though of a pleasant appearance it is a pity that they were made not of Dartmoor granite, but granite from elsewhere. But contrast these to the stones forming a viewing point for the handicapped in the car park at Barn Hill. What a choice of stone here, with raw drill marks and an unsympathetic ensemble!

Having lost the R.A.F. mast on Sharpitor, are we soon to lose the 'television mast' on North Hessary, no longer used for this purpose but only for radio? If so it will be missed by many walkers who use it to orientate themselves!

APPENDIX ONE

Furnum Regis – King's Oven

THE exact location of what the perambulators of 1240 referred to as 'Furnum Regis' still remains in doubt, writers over the past 150 years having given vastly differing accounts of what they believed it to be.

Now known as 'King's Oven', it is marked on the Ordnance Survey maps at SX 674812, to the east of a line drawn between the summit cairn on Watern Hill and the Warren House Inn. This is the supposed site of the royal smelting house where the second smelting took place, a process necessary in the very early tinning days before the introduction of the water-wheel and its ability to provide the power and heat to give white tin at a single smelting. However, in view of the fact that other than this point of reference the only non-natural point mentioned by the perambulators was Siward's Cross (if we include Bronze Age remains for this purpose as 'natural'), it seems not illogical to assume that the summit cairn on Watern Hill was what the perambulators were referring to. Once again, the theory that this summit cairn is, in fact, Furnum Regis, has recently been put forward by Dr Tom Greeves, formerly Archaelogical Officer to the Dartmoor National Park.

It is interesting to review the comments made by past recorders over the years – listed here in order of publication:

Samuel Rowe: *A Perambulation of the Antient and Royal Forest of Dartmoor* (originally published 1848 from observations made in 1825–26).

The original Furnum Regis, the King's Oven, the tin smelting place, was destroyed probably some time during the last century [1700s], and was reduced to further ruin by the removal of stones, or the construction of buildings of Bush Down Mine, which are hard by, but the site is still indicated by a pile of stones, in the midst of a pound that is nearly circular. There are the remains of a rectangular building on the South West side of the pound, and there are also traces of a circle enclosing a cairn, and a kistvaen in the centre. Having exercised our ingenuity, as others have done in endeavouring to find some relics which would account for this curious designation, we proceeded...

Mrs Bray: *The Borders of the Tamar and Tavy* (taken from the 1879 edition: from the 1830s letters of the Rev. Bray).

Sometimes thinking of the burning fiercely furnaces of Nebuchadnezzar, and sometimes of King Arthur's Oven, which I believe is a kind of cromlech in Scotland, I rambled about with an umbrella over my head in search of I know not what. I thought also more than once of a wild goose chase, and almost was induced again and again to give it up; but tempted by the pleasure of exploring unknown regions I persevered.

As I ascended the hill I perceived some ridges of stone, which whether they were the remains of inclosures or tracklines I could not tell. I found an elevated point of view what seemed like the King's broad arrow, which appeared to have but recently made in the turf. And had it not been so long ago, I could have fancied it one of those marks made during the trigonometrical survey by direction of the Ordnance under Colonel Mudge. Soon after I came to something like a small rude circle, with what might have been an erect stone or pillar, but now fallen, and, whether by lightening or otherwise, split longitudinally and laterally into four parts, in nearly equal proportions. Advancing farther, I observed the outline of the summit of the hill

90

somewhat rough with stones and bushes, and hastening towards it found as I conclude the object of my search.

It is a circular barrow composed of small stones, seventy-six paces in circumference. Its form approaches but little too conical, being I should think but three feet high. I saw on it no lichen or moss, which is generally found on structures of this description that have remained in their original form, and I therefore should conclude that many of the stones have at a comparatively late date, been carried away. It can boast of almost a panoramic view of considerable extent, particularly towards the north east and south. Near it is a kind of trench, about six feet long, with a shorter meeting it at right angles in the centre, the sides of which are lined with stone. And in the same direction are several pits, and one in particular of some extent in the shape of an inverted cone.

John Chudleigh: *Devonshire Antiquities* (2nd edition, 1893).

King's Oven, a circular pillar of stones about 3'6" high and 3' diameter, and a flat stone to the pillar. However I cannot see in these any resemblance to an oven, and possibly the pits and trenches on the hill above, near the tumulus, might have rather been so connected.

J. L. W. Page: *An Exploration of Dartmoor*, 1895.

Almost opposite this time-worn relic [Bennett's Cross], a hill rises across the road, crowned by an object mentioned in the Perambulations of 1240 as 'Furnum Regis', and as one of the forest bounds. In it, indeed, we have reached the limit of the east quarter. We ascend the hill to speculate, as many before us have done, on the low cairn, the stone-lined trench, and the little pits, which are all that now remain of what is generally regarded as a smelting house of the old men. I do not however, regard it as anything but a cairn pure and simple, and consider the trench as nothing more or less than a ruined kistvaen. The height of the cairn does not exceed 4 feet. It is crowned with a pile of stones, apparently of recent erection.

Sabine Baring-Gould: *A Book of Dartmoor*, 1900.

Antiently, before the introduction of the wheel, the smelting-place above all others was at King's Oven, or Furnum Regis, near Warren Inn, between Post Bridge and Moreton. It is mentioned in the Perambulation of Dartmoor made in 1240. It consists of a circular enclosure of about 72 yards in diameter, forming a pound, with the remains of a quadrangular building in it. The furnace itself was destroyed some years ago. When the inclosure was made it was carried to a cairn that was in part demolished, to serve to form the bank of the pound. This cairn was ringed about with upright stones, and contained a kistvaen. The latter was rifled, and most of the stones removed to form the walls, but a few of the inclosing uprights were not meddled with, and between two was found firmly wedged a beautiful flint scraper.

William Crossing: *Guide to Dartmoor*, 1912.

It is rather amusing to find the summit of this hill [Watern Hill] described by a writer under the impression that he was giving a reader an account of King's Oven [here Crossing is referring to Page], we venture to think that very few since the days of the Rev E. A. Bray have mistaken Watern Hill for King's Oven...
...about ¼ mile N of the Warren House Inn, shall find ourselves on the site of the ancient blowing-house mentioned in the Perambulation of 1240 as Furnum Regis, and in the Forest Survey of 1609 as King's Oven. In the scanty remains that now exist it would be impossible to recognize the ruins of a smelting house, and it is the name alone that enables us to identify the site. Down to about the second half of the 18th century it would appear that most of this

interesting structure, which in early times was probably the centre of the tin industry in this part of the moor, was standing. Later the work of destruction was completed by the erectors of some modern buildings nearby, who supplied themselves with stone from the ruins. All that is now to be seen is a low rampart, composed of small stones, forming a circular enclosure rather over 700 yards in diameter, in the centre of which is a roughly rounded stone measuring 3 feet across, and near it a small pile of stones that seem to have had one end worked into a rounded form. These were once taken away from the circle to be used in a mine building near by, but before this was done the source whence they had been obtained became known, and they were ordered to be taken back. On the south side of the circle is a delapidated rectangular building, but this cannot with safety be identified as part of the ancient smelting house. Apparently it belongs to a later day than that of the circle. Nothing is known of King's Oven, for the Perambulators of 1240 merely mention it, and do not say whether it was in use at the time. But however this may be we shall hardly be wrong in supposing that its name was derived not from being a furnace connected with tinworks to Henry 3rd but to a much earlier king, for there cannot be a doubt of the high antiquity of this smelting place.

R. Hansford Worth: *Dartmoor*, 1953.

Worth does not refer to the situation of Furnum Regis but quotes:
In each town where there should be a second smelting (not within the walls of Exeter or Bodmin) there was to be one house at the hiring of the king appointed for the second smelting, weighing and stamping, and no one should presume to conduct their operations elsewhere as he valued himself and his goods'.
To this he comments:
...here we have a clue to the Furnum Regis, or King's Oven, near Postbridge, a place appointed for the second smelting 'at the hiring of the king'.

Eric Hemery: *High Dartmoor*, 1983:

Eric Hemery describes the 'pound' or enclosure as 'King's Oven', as others before him, but he also separately describes the cairn on Watern Hill saying:
from its stones on the east side has been built a small shelter; though large enough only for a lookout or shepherd's hut, it is basically of some antiquity and now ruinous. Known as Natty's Castle, the shelter was crudely rebuilt at the outbreak of World War 2.

Thus through a timespan of something like 150 years, comments upon Furnum Regis or 'King's Oven' have been very varied, and at times a little bizarre. But the 'error' of the Rev Bray, supposing the cairn on Watern Hill to be Furnum Regis now seems to be being taken more seriously by Dr Tom Greeves. He has recently propounded that the cairn was indeed the object described in the 1240 Perambulation, and that the low walled passageway on the eastern side of the cairn might represent the entrance to a round chambered tomb, likening this example to others found further afield – not on Dartmoor. The mystery remains!

APPENDIX TWO

Extracts from the
Ordnance Survey Boundary Report Books

SINCE compiling the original text for this book in draft form the author has been fortunate enough to make contact with Mr S. M. Woods, of Porchester, Hants, a very keen Dartmoor enthusiast.

He has been able to examine Boundary Report Books of the years 1882–1883 and has provided photographs of a number of pages which show points of interest in detail, together with some other observations.

The sketches shown in the photographs are here reproduced, with comments by the author, and with due thanks to Mr Woods.

'Property Right':
The 'Property Right' reproduced here is one of many signed by all 'Meresmen', and perhaps dates back to Saxon times and the early enclosure of land.

Chamber's Dictionary defines the word 'mere' as 'a boundary'. 'Merestone' – 'a stone which marks a boundary': thus a 'Meresman' was a person assigned to look after the boundary.

In early times it is recorded that the old hedge banks were formed by building a bank of earth and stone taken from both sides of the finished article, the whole being conducted within the bound of the builder, thus setting the bank within his own property, and also producing many of Devon's old sunken lanes.

Note that the page is signed by James Smerdon, Meresman for Buckland in the Moor, 30 January, 1883.

The Whitmoor Stone:

This point of reference mentioned in the Perambulation of 1240, was known as Parve Hundetorre or Little Hound Tor. The stone, a rough-set stone, is at SX 633890, a short distance from a Stone Circle, and is, in this sketch, described as a 'monolith'. It is interesting to read the note 'Thurlestone or Whitmoor Stone', the former name being an alternative name for Watern Tor, and appears to be misplaced in this instance.

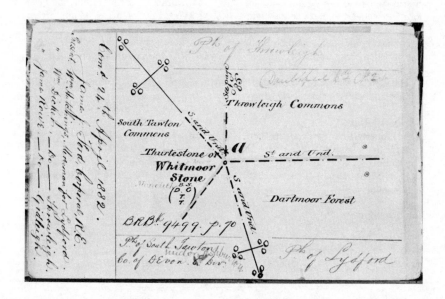

It has several letters inscribed upon it, 'DC' by the Duchy on the south facing side, with the letters 'TP' (Throwleigh Parish) below. The north side, and the narrow east side both have the single letter 'T' for Tawton (South).

The sketch is endorsed 'Parish of Throwleigh, Doubtful Bdy No 2'. It defines the point at which the Forest meets Throwleigh and South Tawton and present at this definition on the 24th April 1882 were: James J. Ford, Corporal, R.E.; Wm Hutchings, Meresman for Lydford; Wm Dicker, – Do – Throwleigh; James Rowe – Do – Gidleigh.

Nun's Cross:

This plan of Nun's Cross is signed by Corp. James J. Ford and thus must date sometime before July 1882, when he became a Sergeant.

It is interesting to note that the Ordnance Survey have used the name 'Nun's Cross' and not Siward's Cross at all times. On the Walkhampton Parish and the Forest (Lydford) bounds, it has been used by the Forest as a boundstone since the original Perambulation of 1240 when it was called by the latter name.

The manuscript note is of interest. It reads 'The boundary runs staight & undefined from Nun's Cross to the boundary stone at Eylesborough'. This line now has plain granite pillars defining it, intermingled with Burrator Reservoir stones.

Note also the spelling of Eylesbarrow, one of the many variants over several centuries.

94

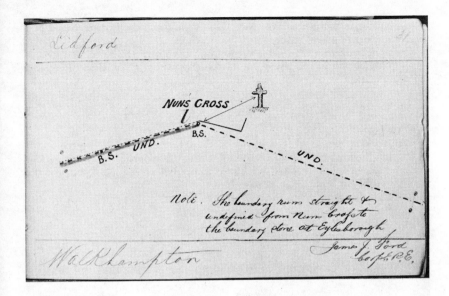

Erme Head area:

This interesting sketch of records by J. J. Ford and dated 6/6/82, shows a part of the boundary common to the Forest (Lydford) and the parishes of Shaugh Prior and Cornwood. Cornwood is shown to be in the 'Southern or Totnes Division', and Shaugh Prior in the 'Western or Tavistock Division'.

It will be noted that the boundary for Cornwood is signed as having been

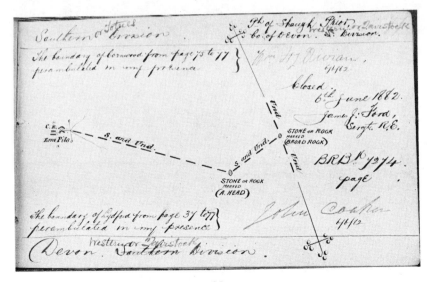

'perambulated in the presence of' Wm. H. J. Vivian, and the Lydford bound in a similar manner by John Coaker.

The stone marked 'A head' is a reference point given in the 1608 Perambulation as 'Arme Headd' and is believed to be the 'Grimsgrove' of 1240. Broad Rock is a manorial stone of Blachford Manor, Cornwood, but, as shown, on the Forest bound.

Watern Tor:

Watern Tor described as the 'Thurlestone' by the perambulators of 1240, is still known as the 'Thirlstone', a term applied to 'holed' stones. It was applied to this tor as, from certain angles, it appears to have such a hole. In reality there is a major portion of the tor separated from a much smaller mass by a gap of a few feet.

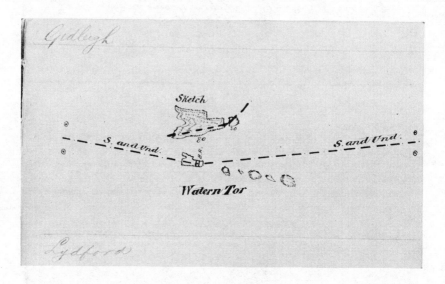

The bound of Gidleigh Parish, here adjoining the Forest bound, passes across this aperture, and it is the practice of the peramulators of the parish to pass through it.

The wall of the main mass, at the point of the bound, is marked with the letters 'GP'. Here the line of the bounds change their line of direction by a few degrees.

Shovel Down and Batworthy Corner:

This sketch dated 14 July 1882, shows an enlargement of the fallen end stones, marked 'Large Stones' at the end of the stone row (double) associated with the Four Fold Circle, prepared by James J. Ford, now Sergeant, R.E.

One of these stones bears the letters 'GP', Gidleigh Parish, but this enlargement clearly shows that the 'turning point' was in reality the centre of the circle.

Cow Bridge, out of the sketch, is still there, but a tithe map also shows another stone very near the corner of the wall at Batworthy Corner (east side).

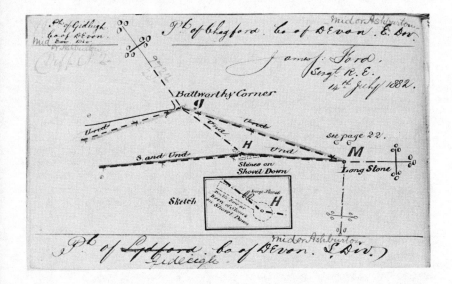

Holne Bounds:

This undated extract shows a stone at Horse Ford, mentioned by William Crossing.

Horse Ford, a crossing place on the O Brook, was on the old monastic route across the moor from Buckfast to Buckland and Tavistock. Until washed away in a violent storm in 1965, one of the stones forming this paved crossing had the letter 'H' engraved upon it – it has now disappeared. See the manuscript note 'The top of the rock is level with the surface of the ground, J.J.F.'.

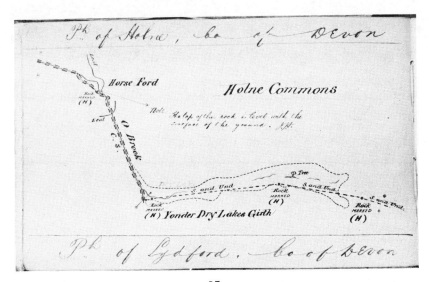

The map also shows other stones marked 'H' up the higher Drylakes Gully, here called 'Yonder Dry Lakes Girth', on the line taking the boundary to Wellaby Gulf and ultimately to Ryder's Hill (Knattleborough). The author has seen of these stones, but they are not marked on the current Ordnance Survey maps.

River Mewy or Meavy:

Now more usually known as the Meavy, but in Crossing's day as the Mew or Mewy, it is here shown as 'Mew', in the early 1880s.

This extract of what is now the area where the Burrator Dam stands, clearly shows the Weir and the 'Plymouth Leat' being taken off, otherwise known as Drake's Leat dating from the sixteenth century. The portion below the dam is still visible today.

Slight differences in the line taken by Sheepstor Parish in the line of their bounds, the main intention of the sketch, are also shown, signed F.E.E. 2nd Corp R.E.

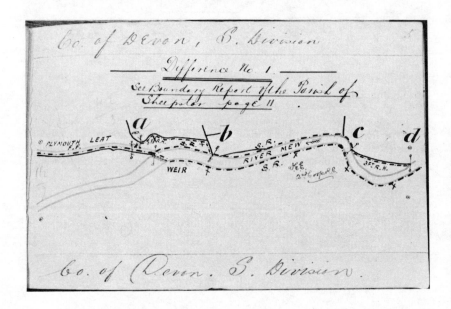

BIBLIOGRAPHY

Albert, W. *Turnpike Road System in England – 1663–1840*. Cambridge U.P., 1972.

Andriette, Eugene A. *Devon and Exeter in the Civil War*. Exeter, 1971.

Cocks, J. Somers. *Devon & Cornwall Notes and Queries* (Vol. 30). 1966.

Crossing, W. *Ancient Crosses of Dartmoor*. Plymouth, 1884.

Crossing, W. *Crossing's Dartmoor Worker*. David & Charles, 1966.

Crossing, W. *Guide to Dartmoor*. David & Charles, 1965.

Crossing, W. *A Hundred Years on Dartmoor*. Plymouth, 1901.

Dymond, R. *Widecombe in the Moor (Things New and Old Concerning, etc.)*. Torquay, 1876.

Ewans, M.C. *The Haytor Granite Tramway and Stover Canal*. David & Charles, 1977.

Gill, Crispin. *Dartmoor: A New Study*. David & Charles, 1970.

Greeves, T. A. P. *The Devon Tin Industry 1450–1750*. (unpublished thesis, 1981).

Haynes, R.G. *Vermin Traps and Rabbit Warrens on Dartmoor*. 1970.

Harris, Helen. *Industrial Archaeology of Dartmoor*. David & Charles, 1968.

Hemery, Eric. *High Dartmoor*. Robert Hale, 1983.

Henderson, C. *Old Devon Bridges*. London, 1938.

Holne, The Villagers of. *A History of Holne*. 1977.

Hoskins, W.G. *Devon*. Collins, 1954.

Hoskins, W.G. *Old Devon*. David & Charles, 1966.

Pennington, R. *A History of the Mining Law of Cornwall and Devon*. London, 1966.

Pilkington, F. *Ashburton, The Dartmoor Town*. Ashburton, 1978.

Rowe, Samuel. *A Perambulation of Dartmoor*. Devon Books, 1985.

Starkey, Harry. *Dartmoor Crosses*. privately published, 1983.

Torr, Cecil. *Small Talk at Wreyland*. O.U.P., 1979.

Worth, R. Hansford. *Dartmoor*. Plymouth, 1953.

Reference has also been made to Ordnance Survey maps of the 1:25 000 scale, the 1:10 000 scale, and the six-inch to the mile scale.

Various volumes of *The Transactions of the Devonshire Association* have been referred to.